HOW THE CHURCHES GOT IT WRONG:

Christianity Revealed

J. Craig Woods

iUniverse, Inc.
Bloomington

How the Churches Got It Wrong:
Christianity Revealed

iUniverse books may be ordered through booksellers or by contacting:

iUniverse
1663 Liberty Drive
Bloomington, IN 47403
www.iuniverse.com
1-800-Authors (1-800-288-4677)

Because of the dynamic nature of the Internet, any web addresses or links contained in this book may have changed since publication and may no longer be valid. The views expressed in this work are solely those of the author and do not necessarily reflect the views of the publisher, and the publisher hereby disclaims any responsibility for them.

Any people depicted in stock imagery provided by Thinkstock are models, and such images are being used for illustrative purposes only.

Certain stock imagery © Thinkstock.

ISBN: 978-1-4759-3134-1 (sc)
ISBN: 978-1-4759-3136-5 (e)

Library of Congress Control Number: 2012910092

Printed in the United States of America

iUniverse rev. date: 6/21/2012

Dedicated to all seekers of truth…

Table of Contents

Introduction

Our Christian religion was created by *men*. Because this is such an obvious statement, it seems unnecessary to be including it here. But maybe it needs to be clearly stated at the outset of our journey into the truth of Jesus Christ. Jesus Christ did not write a single word of print and, in *all* of the gospel accounts, we will not find Jesus Christ issuing creeds and doctrines. Men are solely responsible for the creation of church dogma. If the Christian religion is failing to have a positive impact upon our lives, it is because the Christian religion did not emphasize the love and compassion as found in the Gospel of Jesus Christ. Jesus Christ spent His life teaching a ministry of love and forgiveness. If the message of love is missing from our church's doctrines and dogma, we will need to take a look at the history of our Christian institutions to understand the reasons for this omission. If we are unable to see love and compassion in the behavior of people, who call themselves Christians, we will need to understand the reasons for this omission too. We are now witnessing the introduction of many so-called Christian beliefs and values into our everyday life. This introduction is being executed by the so-called Christian political action groups, as they fervently attempt to influence our government policies. We need to know if their beliefs and values are really consistent with what Jesus of Nazareth taught. We also need to know why the early church leaders were unable to capture the truth, as expressed in the message of Jesus Christ. And the best method for conducting our investigation is to re-visit the actual words of Jesus Christ, as recorded in the Christian Gospels, both canonical and non-canonical Gospels.

However, it is with a certain degree of trepidation that I write a book about the ministry of Jesus Christ and His true message for humanity. Undertaking this journey is, indeed, fraught with many perils for both me and the reader. But I feel it is worth the risk for us to re-examine the message of Jesus Christ, especially as it relates to our current problems. If we are willing to open our eyes and take a penetrating look at our world, we will immediately discern the importance of understanding a message of hope and love, as in the message taught by Jesus Christ. We live in a world beset by many problems, and most of these problems are of our own creation. If we have created these problems, we can solve them. And the message of Christ offers us the solution we need for improving our human condition by providing us with the instructions for the spiritual development of humanity. But if we are to understand what Jesus Christ was—and is—teaching us, we will need to take a new and courageous look at what His message really means for us today. In our renewed pursuit to understand His message, we shall strive to extricate our thinking from the orthodoxy that permeates conventional thinking about the message of Jesus Christ. Long before *men* created the Christian creeds and doctrines of the early Church, Jesus of Nazareth lived amongst the people of His day. His mission was to teach a ministry of love without judgment and condemnation. Within the Gospels, we will not find any examples of Jesus Christ creating creeds or doctrines, which are now central in the worship practiced by our modern Christian institutions. There is no condemnation in the message of Jesus Christ. The message of Christ is all about unconditional love and this love is all inclusive. This is the love that God has for man—and this love was made manifest by the appearance of the Christ Spirit in our human world. Unfortunately, by focusing on the creation of dogma, our Christian institutions are missing the essential message of love and compassion, as found in the message of Jesus Christ.

This current work constitutes a major revision to my previous book, *A New Age of Vision*. In this new book, I have kept the basic premise, but I have revised every chapter by changing the structure and adding new material. I was able to learn much in writing my previous book. For one thing, I have learned that you must be very careful in choosing your title. The title must reflect the essence of your book, but you must be careful not to turn people away by what you choose. I have chosen the bold title, *How the Churches Got It Wrong: Christianity Revealed*, with the purpose of indicating that institutional Christianity has been unable to have a significant impact upon the prevention of man's inhumanity to man such as we see manifested in our wars, famine and poverty. On the contrary, we have seen the greatest examples of these transgressions in countries that claim to be Christian societies. In addition, the Roman Church, which held sway over the western world for about fifteen-hundred years, has been one of the most persistent violators of the principles Jesus Christ espoused. In seeking to establish their ecclesiastical authority over all other institutions, the Roman Church ignored the simple words of love and compassion spoken by the man from Galilee. And this very same omission of love and compassion from the Gospel of Jesus Christ has also occurred in the other Christian institutions such as Protestantism and Evangelism. Because of the greed and corruption in the Roman Church, the Protestants would separate from the Church of Rome during the sixteenth century, but, unfortunately, they would also carry out their own brutal policy of subjugation. When it comes to creating Christian institutions, it appears that the goal of unconditional love, as expressed by Jesus of Nazareth, is conspicuously absent.

The Gospel of Jesus Christ is about how we are to love God and love one another. It is a message of peace, hope and love and, as such, it is *not* a message of judgment and condemnation. But the early Church opted for the creation of institutional authority and worldly power. The early Church leaders would literally go from being persecuted to being the persecutors. Consequently, the message of love taught by Jesus of Nazareth has been unable to take root in our society. By writing this book, I sincerely hope that I will, in some small measure, assist in correcting this egregious error. Mohandas Gandhi once asked why Christians "are so unlike your Christ?" To find a reasonable answer to his query, we will need to make a thorough investigation into the institutions that claim to espouse the message of Jesus Christ. Because our Christian institutions have overlooked the message of love and compassion in their distorted interpretation of the Gospel of Jesus Christ, we will need to search for the truth that has been buried under verbal abstractions. Our Christian institutions have been mainly interested in material acquisition, instead of the salvation of humanity through unconditional love. Unfortunately, their distortions have significantly influenced our perceptions of Christianity. In their misguided efforts, these institutions have created belief systems that most people believe are antagonistic to their lifestyle. If ever a spiritual journey was needed, it is now that we should undertake our most important journey. It will be our spiritual journey to discover the truth about our human existence, as taught by Jesus Christ. While traveling on our journey, we shall also learn how we can begin to develop our love for our brothers and sisters.

I would also hasten to add that my understanding of the Christ message, as expressed in this book, is not a new understanding. The message of Christ was a new Gospel for humanity at the time when Jesus Christ expressed it two thousand years ago. Since the time of Jesus Christ, there have been various individuals who have made progress in understanding His message—and this understanding will form the basis for this book. Unfortunately, their voices have been unable to rise above the din of orthodoxy. I am not quite sure why I think this current work will fare any better but, with the many problems we are now experiencing, I feel the time is right for us to re-visit the message that Jesus Christ brought to earth. My extensive research into the history of Christianity and my background in the formal academic studies of world religions, psychology and philosophy have provided me with an unique ability to offer a comparative view of Christian theology. I have spent a number of years in the pursuit of understanding the history and development of Christian theology—and I have studied the various philosophical schools that have exerted their influence on the development of Christianity such as Platonism. A few of the Church Fathers, including Saint Augustine, were avid students of Plato's philosophy, which would have a major influence on their views about the message of Christ.

The message of Christ offers us the truth we need for our tumultuous times, but this truth has been largely ignored and, subsequently, lost. If we are to pursue our spiritual development, our materialistic pursuits must eventually be supplanted by spiritual learning, and the message of Jesus Christ provides us with the instructions for learning the spiritual purpose for our human existence. While our technological gadgets provide us with a false sense of security, our souls languish in a place of spiritual desolation. And with technology about to overtake our humanity, we must at last return to our true purpose: the care and development of our spiritual being. My sincere desire is for this book to be of assistance to all seekers who are interested in finding the spiritual path to truth. I wrote this book so that we could search for the truth as we journey together. In the final analysis, only the person who is willing to take this journey will be in the position to render their judgment on how helpful this book has been for seeking truth in his or her life.

First and foremost, this is a philosophical book about unconditional love. In our journey, we will explore the unlimited potential of having a loving attitude, as expressed in the message of Jesus Christ. As most of us know, Jesus Christ never wrote a single word of His message. And the Christian Gospels were written many decades after His death. The narrative contained within the Gospels was originally passed on in the oral tradition until it was expressed on the written page. As such, we may not conclude that the Gospels are infallible. However, these accounts of Jesus Christ are all we have to go on. They provide us with a second-hand account of His life and His message, and they will help us in understanding His ministry of love. Because of a discovery in the twentieth century, we can also utilize other Christian Gospels for our understanding of His ministry. These Christian Gospels were excluded from the New Testament Bible Canon for reasons we shall explore later in our journey. With these recently found Christian Gospels and the New Testament Gospels, we will be able to glean the essence of the message that Jesus of Nazareth was disseminating to the people. And they will provide us with a substantial understanding of His ministry. As we shall see, the central theme in all the Gospels is a message of love: loving God and loving one another. There are no examples or quotes in which we will find Jesus Christ creating church doctrines or dogma. Church leaders would perform the task of creating our Christian theology many years after the death of Jesus Christ. In so doing, these men laid the foundation for modern Christianity. Although the central theme in the message of Jesus Christ is all about love, we will need to develop a new understanding of how Jesus Christ envisioned the concept of love. And we can do this by understanding how the word love is used in the Gospels. To do this, we will investigate the language used in writing the New Testament, specifically the New Testament Gospels.

Originally written in Greek, the New Testament writers actually used three different Greek words for the concept of love, and their usage depends on the context in which they are found. Most of our English translations use our English word "love" in translating the Greek word used for love in the Biblical Gospels. In these Gospels, the most common Greek word used for our English word "love" is the Greek word "agape." In understanding the message of love in the ministry of Jesus of Nazareth, it will be important to understand the meaning of the Greek term "agape." Agape is the highest form of love. It is unconditional and self-sacrificing love for a person or object because we realize this person or object is very precious to us. Agape is unselfish love, and its meaning is nearer in meaning to our English word "altruism." The type of love alluded to by Jesus of Nazareth is the highest expression of love. To a certain degree, the love expressed by Jesus Christ cannot be defined. It is the love that characterizes God's relationship with humanity and, like the concept of God, it is an inexpressible idea. The meaning of love, as used by Jesus Christ in his Gospel of Truth, has a dynamic nature to it. This kind of love is evolving as we evolve. The potential of this love (agape) is unlimited. True Christianity is to be founded on this kind of love, and it will have no need for anything else because this love is the Power of God. In the journey that we are about to undertake, it will be our goal to travel as far as possible in comprehending the ultimate expression of love. It is my sincere hope that we will realize our goal and, thusly, we will find a more spiritual basis for living together and loving one another.

On our journey, we will explore the history of the Christian religion, and we shall see specific examples of how men created the Christian doctrines that are now at the core of our Christian institutions. With this information, we may better understand why the Christian religion is failing us. I will accomplish this investigation by referring to the canonical Gospels found in the New Testament Bible. And I will also explore the other Christian Gospel books that were excluded from the New Testament Bible Canon. While these excluded gospels were extremely popular amongst the early Christians, they were, unfortunately, excluded from the Christian Bible Canon. And this was largely due to the politics and personalities of the early Church leaders, who created our Christian religion. Many of these non-canonical Christian Gospels were discovered at an Egyptian site near the village of Nag Hammadi in 1945. I will also rely on other ancient religious texts that would have been known to, and read by, the people who lived during that time when men were creating the Christian religion. Some of these ancient texts will come from a body of literature known as the *Corpus Hermeticum*. As we shall see, these Hermetic books would influence some of the leading Christian thinkers throughout the ages. I shall also utilize concepts from classical literature, as well as ideas from science and philosophy. In so doing, I hope to weave together an exciting exposition of what Jesus Christ was really teaching us. We will travel together on what I hope is a spirited journey—a journey that is both personal and meaningful for all who are courageous enough to undertake it.

Although it will be necessary to include a brief discussion about early Christian history, this book is not intended to be an academic history book on Christianity. There are many scholastic books on this subject available for anyone seeking a formal study of Christianity. Some of these academic studies of Christianity are very good, and some are a bit arid and tedious. However, it is my intention to take us on a personal journey of discovery. This will be a journey of discovery to find the purpose for the appearance of Jesus Christ in our physical world. And it will provide us with a re-interpretation of His message. It will also be a journey about us—both as individuals and as a society. It is a journey into the nature of truth: truth about the reason for our existence. In considering the extremely daunting nature of such a journey, I humbly hope that I have achieved some of my goals. In my mind, I cannot envision any valid reasons for why the greatest message of hope for humanity should be lacking in excitement and joy. In fact, the joy of discovery is at the core of the Gospel of Jesus Christ.

Any discussion about finding a path to peace, love and joy is certainly a discussion of the greatest importance for us in our time—or at any time. The path we seek is nothing less than the path to heaven. By "heaven," I mean—as Jesus Christ meant—a spiritual paradise here on earth and beyond. My sincere hope is to explore the message of Christ by having a lively, provocative, and enthralling discussion about the *most* important truth that has ever been revealed to humanity. Jesus Christ taught us that our human spirit is the divine spark from God and this is our true self. Jesus Christ was expressing this reality when He stated "God is within us." Because we are so preoccupied with the demands of a modern materialistic world, most of us have neglected or have been unable to learn about the true purpose for our existence. Our true purpose for descending into the physical world is for the spiritual growth of our human spirit. Our spiritual development is the raison d'être for our existence. Our journey in this book will be our exploration into the spiritual realm of the human spirit, and we will base our conclusions upon the wisdom of Christ, as shared by Jesus Christ Himself, the *real* founder of Christianity.

The major impediment to understanding a book of this type may be found in our attitude. There are typically two attitudes that a person may bring to a new book, especially a book that professes to explore a topic as controversial as the message of Jesus Christ. One of these attitudes is characterized by having a closed mind. This person will immediately put the book down as soon as they encounter an idea or a concept that they do not agree with. If our minds are closed, there is indeed very little we will ever learn. The second type of attitude is displayed by the person who looks for any kind of evidence in the new book that will confirm their existing beliefs and opinions. This person is at risk of missing new and vital information because their only objective is to confirm what they already knew. Both of these attitudes will keep us from learning new information—and this new information could possibly help us to achieve elevated spiritual awareness and thereby save our lives.

In His Gospel, Jesus Christ provided us with the best possible insight for understanding His message. He tells us that we must attempt to understand His message with a childlike mind. The childlike mind possesses the openness and trust that are necessary for apprehending His truth. A child's mind has not yet developed prejudice. With a receptive and willing attitude, we will be able to learn the spiritual lessons that Jesus Christ is revealing to us. If we actually listen to His message with "new" ears, Jesus Christ is truly revealing the instructions for humanity to enter the kingdom of heaven. Could we possibly ask for more? An attitude of openness and willingness will also allow us to discern the difference between church dogma and spiritual enlightenment. Attitude is our mindset—and our mindset dictates the direction in which we will move. Our attitude is the mainspring for our actions—and our thinking will determine our attitude. If any individual, with an open mind, honestly weighs this book and finds that it is deficient, I can readily accept this result. However, the importance of our attitude cannot be over emphasized. And if we are to learn how to develop an attitude that allows us to be teachable, we will need to understand the instrument that creates our attitude—and this instrument is our mind. With the interplay between thoughts and emotions, we establish our own attitude toward our inner self and the outer world. Everything we do in life starts with our attitude (mindset). Developing an attitude that is conducive to learning is our first lesson in our search for spiritual growth. We will explore the subject of attitude and mind in greater detail in our upcoming journey.

I would also like to add a few words about language. When attempting to understand God's purpose for us—as we will attempt to do on this journey—we will inevitably confront metaphysical and spiritual matters. Unfortunately, English is ill-equipped to express such matters. I have tried to render our subject with as much clarity as is possible. When a new term or concept is introduced, I have tried to define this new term or concept at the time of its introduction. I have, as well, attempted to maintain a consistent definition with the future use of these terms and concepts. My fellow travelers on this journey will be the final judges of my success or failure. We may be well served if we remember that we are dealing with complicated abstractions—and sometimes the best method for understanding these abstractions is to re-read difficult sentences and paragraphs. Heaven knows, I frequently went back to rewrite many of these descriptions in the hope of finding consistency, precision and clarity.

Throughout our journey, one of my central themes is to present the case that the foundation for modern Christianity was laid down with the beginning of the Church of Rome. If we inspect our current Christian theology, we will see that many of the beliefs were developed at the beginning of the Roman Church. Although these original beliefs may now vary slightly from church to church, they are, in one form or another, the same fundamental principles taught by most of our modern churches. Dogmatic beliefs such as "Jesus Christ is God," "The Trinity," "Original Sin" and "The Fall" have all made their way into the current Christian theology, and they are expressed from most pulpits. Even when the Unitarian Churches oppose the dogma of the Trinitarian Churches, they are doing so based on concepts originally developed over eighteen-hundred years ago. There is, indeed, not much new under the Sun. Also, throughout our journey, I will frequently use the terms "Church" or "Great Church." These terms are intended to be collective terms that include most Christian institutions taken as a single totality. We may think of these terms as meaning Christendom. When appropriate, I will indicate particular churches by using their specific names, such as the Roman Church.

The Christian religion was created by men in the first few centuries after the death of Jesus Christ and, as such, it is heavily stressed with male dominance. Sadly, this male dominance is about the same in our modern times. This reality is clearly illustrated by the largest Christian sect, the Church of Rome, in their refusal to allow women to become priests. I cannot, in good conscience, write about God using male pronouns. The use of such male pronouns only adds to the already existing obscuration that surrounds the nature of God the Great Spirit, our Father, who has created all we know and all we will ever know. But finding a suitable term for referring to God is impossible. So, when referring to God, I have simply chosen the convention of using a combination of the male and female pronouns, such as "His-Her," where possible and when they make sense. However, I have kept the tradition of referring to the Christ Spirit as a male entity. This makes sense in my mind because He lived amongst us as the man known to us as Jesus of Nazareth, the male child of Mary and Joseph.

Our journey will begin with a very brief history on how men created Christianity. This history will allow us to understand how we have arrived at our current interpretation of Christianity and how His message has become distorted. This historical perspective is necessary for understanding how the Christian creeds and doctrines, which are now central to current Christian theology, were created by men for the incipient Church. But I must stress that this history of the early Church is very brief, and for those individuals desiring greater details, they will find some excellent histories of Christianity in the bibliography at the end of this book. I found it exceedingly fascinating to learn about the process of how Christianity was created. It is vital for us to understand how important a role personality and politics played in the process of formulating creeds and doctrines for the new Christian religion. There was nothing Godly about the process. I think the individuals who are undertaking this journey will be as fascinated as I was to learn that most of these doctrines are not found in the Christian Bible, the New Testament. And they most certainly do *not* find expression in the words of Jesus Christ.

A few words of caution may be appropriate for understanding why chapter 2 has been included. In this chapter, our journey takes a turn into a discussion about the nature of our mind. At first, this may appear as though the chapter is a digression from our topic. However, in our attempt to answer such questions as "How are we to understand the Christ message?" and "What did Jesus Christ *really* mean to tell us?" we will need to have a deeper understanding of the instrument that performs the function of understanding. And this instrument is our mind. Our mind is responsible for understanding the truth of Jesus Christ. Understanding the nature of our mind as a vehicle for thought that is separate from, but connected to, our physical body is fundamental to our spiritual journey. By investigating our mind, we will begin to know ourselves, as Jesus Christ knows us—as beings with a human spirit and a physical body connected by a mind. It is the mind that allows the human spirit to impart movement to the physical body. The mind provides the connection between the spiritual and physical realms.

In an attempt to effectively explore the nature of our mind, chapter 2 will include different concepts derived from the study of science, psychology and philosophy. In addition to our exploration into the mind and human consciousness, we shall also explore the fallacy that Christianity is in opposition to modern science. If the Christ message is about the truth, this opposition needs to be debunked. The fallacious notion of opposition has been artificially and arbitrarily introduced by the *men* of both the Church and science. And the apparent antagonism between Christianity and science has been created by our ignorance of the true message of Jesus Christ. We will explore this topic in depth during our trip into the world of thought. Again, I hasten to add, this is not a technical textbook about scientific concepts. When it became necessary to investigate some of these formal scientific concepts, my overriding concern was with brevity and clarity. While I attempted a distillation of these complex concepts, my true goal was to capture their essence and their relevance for our spiritual journey. Again, the journeyer will be the final judge of my success or failure.

After we explore the historical development of Christianity—and after our investigation into the world of thought—we will spend the remainder of this book on our journey to find the path leading to truth, wisdom and love, as found in the message of Christ. It is my hope that we will investigate His message as though we are spiritual archeologists, digging for the truth that has remained buried under two-thousand years of obfuscation. Regardless of our religious background—and in spite of its resulting religious bias—may we all agree, at this early stage of our journey, that the appearance of Jesus Christ in our human world was, indeed, a very special and unique event in the history of humanity? Whatever our thoughts are about Jesus Christ, we can surely admit that His message of perfect love is unique in the annals of humanity, and it may be our only path through all the worldly madness we are now experiencing on a daily basis. If what the renowned psychiatrist Thomas Szasz says is true when he asserts "There is no such thing as insanity, there are only people half adjusting to an insane world," then we are again reminded of the importance of finding a path that will lead us to our psychological and spiritual growth. And, in the journey we are about to undertake, we shall discover that these two aspects of human growth are actually one and the same. Truthfully, we will discover a new understanding of Jesus Christ. Our new understanding will radically change our perception both of our world and ourselves. Our journey will follow the spiritual path that leads us to the wisdom of Jesus Christ. And His wisdom includes all the other diverse variations of wisdom that have been splintered throughout our world in various forms. We may all travel on different roads, but if the road we are travelling on does not lead to the place of love (agape), we are most likely on the wrong road. As Jesus Christ said, "The truth shall set you free." If our journey yields no results other than our development of Christian mansuetude, it will have been well worth our time. May your journey be blessed with the love of God and the truth of Jesus Christ!

A Gathering of Wise Men

In the beginning, Man created God; and in the image of Man created He him.

And Man gave unto God a multitude of names that he might be God over all the earth when it was suited to Man.

And on the seven millionth day, Man rested and did lean heavily on his God and saw that it was good.

And Man became the God that he had created and with his miracles did rule over all the earth.

—Jethro Tull, Aqualung Album Note, 1971

Men make gods and worship their creation. It would be better for the gods to worship human beings.

—The Gospel of Philip, Nag Hammadi Library

I think that any modern examination of Christianity must first begin with the all important question that Joan O'Grady posits in her excellent book entitled *Early Christian Heresies*: "Has Christianity grown in the way its founder intended and has it kept to its true course?" While this question lies at the heart of our journey, it is, nonetheless, a very difficult question to answer. One of the immediate problems that come to mind is how do we determine the intentions of Jesus Christ and what sources do we use to derive these determinations. After some two thousand years, it has become exceedingly difficult to discern truth from error by investigating the doctrines and dogmas

1

that were created by *men* whose interpretations were frequently based upon various political and social agendas. These agendas were often the result of the civil, social and political conditions of the times in which these men lived. These obstacles render our search for the truth in the message of Christ elusive. Notwithstanding, we can be certain that at Christianity's earliest times, starting with Saint Paul— sometimes referred to as the first theologian of Christianity—*men* were making their religious interpretations based upon their personal beliefs and preferences. And these inclinations were a function of the social and political climate of the first few centuries of the Common Era. Consequently, their religious constructs reflected their personal concerns and values. In addition, these religious interpretations were also filtered through their own individual psychology as first-, second- and third-century men. While these conditions may not necessarily negate the totality of the early Christian interpretations, they do, however, allow us to ask our question about the harmony of these interpretations with the intent of Jesus Christ.

If we were to strip away the last nineteen hundred years of all our technological advances and place ourselves back in the first century just after the crucifixion of Jesus Christ, we would discover that we are exceedingly similar to the people living during this time period. They were preoccupied with the same issues and concerns that preoccupy us today. People at this time—as are people now— were concerned about their family's well-being; they were concerned about their economic conditions; they were concerned about a government that was encroaching upon their personal freedoms. In many respects, our emotional evolution has not separated us— to any significant degree—from our ancestry. We would certainly understand their fears, their desires and their need for physical and emotional security. We would, however, find the religious ethos of these early times very different from our current times. On the whole, first-century denizens were very serious about their beliefs pertaining to God (or gods) and their different methods of worshiping their God (or gods). This preoccupation with God was pervasive in their daily existence. Talk at the marketplace would often revolve around religious themes. And this reality would be most evident in the small backwater province of the Roman Empire known as Judea.

During the middle of the first century, the imperial government of Rome, headed by Emperor Vespasian, was struggling to impose Roman law and order on the Jewish population of Judea. The Jews were a fiercely independent people and by the middle of the first century an all-out rebellion against Rome was being waged by the Jewish people of Judea. In 70 CE, a Roman army under the leadership of the emperor's son, Titus, finally crushed this revolt and destroyed most of the city of Jerusalem, including the destruction of the Jewish Second Temple. At this time, the Christian Jews—those Jews that had become early converts to the Jesus Christ movement—believed the war to be a preliminary to the Second Coming of their Christ. Therefore, they did not participate in the revolt against Rome. Their withdrawal from this conflict engendered intense hostility among their fellow Jews who had fought and lost, but survived this transformative conflict. From this point on, Jewish conversions to Christianity were seriously curtailed. But it is during this time that Saint Paul was working his magic amongst the Gentiles of the Roman Empire.

These were the turbulent times in which the young religion of Christianity was attempting to become a universally established Christian Church. It was also a dangerous time to openly confess your faith in the man from Galilee. Paul is one of the first persons to realize the importance of disseminating his Christian ideas to non-Jews and he would begin to develop a global Christian Church. Paul also created most of the early Christian theology for his early converts. The Apostle Peter may also be given credit for spreading his teacher's word to Rome and Mark the Evangelist is to be given credit for his work in Egypt. The Apostle Thomas is unique in that he took the message of Christ to India, but it is Paul who has been given credit for doing most of the early legwork in the dissemination of early Christianity.

When we consider Paul as Christianity's first theologian, we are struck with the idea of how unlikely an individual he was for this task. To begin with, he never met Jesus of Nazareth in the flesh. He had a solid Hellenized education and he was a Roman citizen. Before becoming Christianity's first itinerant preacher, he was a vehement conservative and he was involved in persecuting the early

Christians. But all of this changed after he had his conversion to the early Jesus movement. His conversion was due to a mystical vision he experienced of the Risen Christ. This conversion illustrates Paul's acquisition of a new spiritual vision of life. And from this point on, he was to travel throughout most of the Roman Empire, disseminating his brand of Pauline Christianity. His letters (epistles) to the various cities, which he was attempting to Christianize, are among the oldest books in the Christian Bible, the New Testament. These books help form the foundation for the later development of Christian theology. Paul was both very passionate and persuasive in his proselytical work. But his real genius was in his ability to codify *his understanding* of Christianity, and to offer his version of Christian standards to non-Jews. This ability helped him develop a network of churches that began to coalesce around a collection of common standards and beliefs. When these early Christian communities experienced problems or controversies, Paul was able to provide the answers that offered solutions to their issues. Of course, these answers were based on Paul's understanding of what he thought Jesus Christ was teaching while He walked the earth. This does not necessarily mean that Paul was wrong or right in his understanding of the message of Christ. It does indicate Paul was providing the early converts with his own interpretation and understanding of the Christ message. Paul was, in many ways, representative of a first-century Middle Eastern man, including his views about how women should hold an inferior role in this new church. We need to understand that Pauline Christianity was based on Paul's understanding of the nature of Jesus Christ and what He represented. To understand Paul's interpretation of the message of Christ, it is important that we first understand who Paul was, what he believed his mission to be, and how he conducted his mission. The Bible Gospels were yet to appear and the only doctrines of belief for early Christians were the beliefs that Paul was disseminating to the early Christian Church communities outside the area of Palestine.

At this early stage of the Jesus movement, there were no established doctrines or creeds. As Paul traveled throughout the Roman Empire, outside of area of Judea, he was disseminating his understanding of the message of Christ. And there are, indeed, some very beautiful ideas expressed in the letters of Saint Paul. Having never met Jesus of Nazareth in the flesh, Paul's experience of Jesus Christ came from his spiritual vision and his subsequent epiphany. Therefore, his perception of Jesus Christ gave him a more mystical interpretation of the message of Christ. Apostles such as Peter, Andrew, Thomas and James, having experienced the living Christ, based their perceptions on a more literal foundation. While Paul was converting the Gentiles, Peter and James would continue to serve the Jesus movement in the area of Jerusalem. They would emphasize a more Jewish approach to their Jesus movement. Possibly, due to his mystical experience of the Risen Jesus Christ, Paul was able to realize that the essential element in the message of Christ is love. Therefore, Paul's ministry invariably emphasized this message of love. Paul's spiritual vision allowed him to understand that all people, Gentiles and Jews, are worthy of redemption. Without a doubt, Paul is certainly worthy of our praise and adulation for both his devoutness and his undying love for Jesus Christ. While history cannot investigate Paul's "vision," it does, however, record that something very profound must have occurred to cause this man to radically alter his life. Notwithstanding, we need to understand that the message he brought to the early Christian communities was filtered through his Hellenized education and through the personal psychology of a *man* living in the first century. But, nonetheless, his interpretation of the message of Christ began to form the foundation for the young Christian Church.

During the first six centuries of the Common Era, the Christian creeds and doctrines were created and defined by the men of the Roman Church. After the sixth century, developmental changes would continue, but these would be more of an administrative type—as opposed to the doctrinal developments of the first six centuries. The early development of the Roman Church is nothing less than miraculous. Church leaders would literally go from being the persecuted to being the persecutors. Christianity would make its debut in an environment filled with both danger, and many competing religious systems. We often overlook the fact that Christianity did not begin as a single monolithic movement. There were many different sects of Christianity in the beginning. And it did not evolve in an environment devoid of other religious beliefs. In addition to

Judaism, there were already an abundance of successful religions being practiced in the Middle East and in the larger Roman world. Religions such as Greco-Roman theology, Mithraism, Zoroastrianism, Neo-Platonism, Hermetic theosophy and other lesser known local religious systems were enjoying much success with the people of the Roman Empire at the time of Jesus Christ. Gnosticism would also begin to emerge on the scene during this period and, because of its importance to the development of Christianity, we will take a closer look at it later in this chapter. Also, during the third century, you can add Manichaeism into the mix of religions competing with nascent Christianity. The attraction of Manichaeism was so appealing to Saint Augustine that he first became a Manichean before he opted for Christianity. As Christianity grew in the first few hundred years, the multitude of different influences on it would result in various Christian interpretations and different Christian churches. The early Christian environment was, indeed, very rich and diverse and there was no dominate church. If we had been alive at the start of the third century CE, it would have been impossible to know the particular sect of Christianity that would emerge as the dominant form of Christianity.

Without a doubt, the single most important event that would allow the early Roman Church to win the high-stakes competition was the "Edict of Milan." This proclamation was made by the Roman Emperor in 313 CE. With this edict, Emperor Constantine declared that all Christians would officially have the liberty to follow their religion as they saw fit without any more persecution. The historical significance of this event for Christianity cannot be overstated. It is very difficult to imagine the fate of Christianity without this intervention by the Roman Emperor. After the death of Emperor Diocletian, with yet another power struggle breaking out in the Roman Empire, General Constantine was able to ascend to the highest level of Roman power by winning a series of battles. Eusebius, the fourth-century Church historian, heresiologist and Bishop of Caesarea, in his *Ecclesiastical History*, claimed that Constantine, just before a crucial battle, had seen a vision of a flaming cross that appeared in the sky. And, in his vision, this cross was inscribed with the words "by this, conquer." General Constantine employed the symbol of the Christian cross on his army's standards and he went on to win this critical battle. This victory allowed Constantine to become the emperor of the Roman Empire. And his mystical vision appears to have influenced Emperor Constantine in his support for Christianity. While history cannot prove the veracity of this story written by Eusebius, the story did effectively serve the early Christian cause. Upon becoming emperor, he moved his seat of power from Rome to the old city of Byzantium. He renamed it Constantinople, giving rise to what history has recorded as the Byzantine Empire. Moving the seat of power from Rome to Constantinople also gave rise to what historians call the Eastern Roman Empire, which would survive the fall of the Western Roman Empire in the fifth century. The Eastern Roman Empire would survive for another millennium—until the Ottoman Turks brought it down in the fifteenth century.

When Christianity was officially declared a legal religion in the Roman Empire, it was time to precisely define what Christianity would be and what it would not be. This would prove to be no easy task. Emperor Constantine's hope that a single religion would help unify his kingdom was woefully unfounded. To begin with, there had been a plethora of competing ideas about the nature of Jesus Christ, and what He had taught, emerging during the first, second and third centuries. There were also controversies about His purpose for coming to earth. Within Constantine's kingdom, conflict was rife about this enigmatic preacher from the Galilee. And serving as an indication of how problematic it would be to define Christianity, the first and most important problem confronting these early leaders of the incipient Roman Church was to define exactly *who* was Jesus Christ. If they were going to have a viable Christian religion, these early Church leaders would need to define Jesus of Nazareth. And, unfortunately, Jesus did not leave these men any documentation about who He was. All they had were some vague references written by men decades after His departure. These references included the "Son of God" and the even more arcane reference the "Son of Man," and these references were not long on description. In their attempts to define Jesus Christ and His mission, the patristic theologians and bishops of the early Roman Church would spend the fourth, fifth and sixth centuries fighting over the definition of Christianity. And these Christological disputes would become very acrimonious. It was during these centuries when *men* created the Christian religion and, in so doing, they created the doctrines and creeds that are still central to modern Christianity. It is not difficult to understand why some have suggested that when Christianity was recognized as the official religion of the Roman Empire, it ceased to be Christianity.

Before the Edict of Milan, Christianity—and the worship by its believers—would have appeared very different from the Christianity we see today. Most churches would have been located in one of the houses where a Christian resided, possibly a leader in the community. Early Christian communities would have been an environment where members shared all of their possessions, including food. The early converts would have found these Christian communities to be a place of support for both their physical and spiritual needs. Early Christianity was also known to be a religion that made great demands on those who wished to follow its path. It could take several years of training before the catechumen was accepted into the body of practicing Christians. Christian ethics required a higher standard of behavior than the normal custom of the time. But all of this changed when Christianity was elevated to legal status in the Roman Empire. Christianity now became a sign of respectability for those wanting to advance in the Roman society. The church edifice would now become the central place for worship. And with a higher status in the Church came much greater power for the individual. Also, Christian standards would now need to be relaxed so that Christianity's mass appeal would be increased and, consequently, the Roman Church could grow in attendance. With the beginning of legal Christianity, the Church leaders had to enter into a kind of Faustian covenant: they would get their Great Church, but the central power for this developing Church would be the temporal leader of the Roman Empire, the Roman Emperor. The early Church began to resemble Imperial Rome by incorporating its legal system when dealing with such issues as regulating punishment and rewards. It was the beginning of a thousand-year reign of absolute Church power.

During the first three centuries, before the church formulated their orthodox creeds and doctrines concerning Christological and soteriological issues, many competing Christian ideas and concepts were expressed by the various Christian churches. Beginning with the Apostles, there were early disputes about what Christianity should or should not be. For example, we find ample evidence for disagreements between Peter and Paul expressed in Paul's epistle, the Book of Galatians. The Apostle Paul was mainly concerned with a less Jewish and more Gentile form of Christianity. Pauline Christianity would be oriented for the people of new lands and new cultures outside the area of Judea. Opposing Paul on some of these new views were the Apostles Peter and James. The Apostle James was the brother (or possibly half-brother) of Jesus Christ and, as such, he carried significant weight within the Jerusalem Christian sect. Peter and James based their Jerusalem Christian sect more on Jewish laws and Jewish customs. Paul was quick to understand that many Gentiles were interested in a new form of Christianity that would be separate from Judaism.

Amid the many growing divisions, Christianity would also confront its first major controversy, and this conflict would be introduced by a Christian presbyter. Arius was a third-century poet and ascetic priest residing in Alexandria, Egypt. In his definition of Jesus Christ, Arius postulated that the Son could not be greater than the Father. He went on to say that the Father created the Son and, therefore, Christ the Son could not be the same (consubstantial) entity as God the Father. It had been during the second century that the concept of the Trinity first began to evolve from a short and nebulous passage found in the Gospel of Matthew. (Matthew 28:19) An early example of the conflict concerning the Trinity can be found in the third century when it had become a source of disputation between the Gnostic Christians and the third century Church Father, Origen of Alexandria. Now, with Arius jumping into the fray, it became a full-blown conflict throughout the whole empire. For us today, it is difficult to imagine how a theological dispute would have occupied the public life of most of the citizens but this was exactly the case for the people of the first centuries in the Common Era. Maybe it will help us to understand the intensity of this dispute if we think about it in terms of the disputes we see today between Republicans and Democrats.

The question of who is Jesus Christ constitutes the most central issue in Christianity. However, the major problem with this question—as was the problem with most of these early theological disputes—is that there are no precise scriptural definitions to be found in the New Testament that can be used to base Church doctrines upon. In the Gospels of the New Testament, Jesus Christ is teaching us *how* to live and *how* to love. He is not defining creed or doctrine for us. The Church's need for a precise definition of Jesus Christ would necessitate the First World (Ecumenical) Council to be convened. In developing a Christian institution, precise verbal definition was needed. These Christological disputes were renting the empire and Emperor Constantine felt that he had to put a stop to what he called "nonsense." So the emperor called forth the wise men to convene and to create the doctrines for his new Church.

The Council of Nicaea was convened in 325 CE, at the city of Nicaea, in modern-day Turkey. It was attended by one hundred bishops from Asia Minor, seventy bishops from Syria and Phoenicia, twenty bishops from Palestine and Egypt, and a few from the Latin West, including two priest-delegates from Rome. Emperor Constantine presided over this august assemblage and the template for solving future theological controversies would be set in place. It was at this council that we find the first use of the Greek term *homoousios*—of one substance—being employed to define the relationship between Jesus Christ and God. This concept was proposed in opposition to the Greek term *homoiousius*—of like substance, but not of the same. This term also appears for the first time, and it sums up the view of Jesus Christ expressed by Arius and his followers. With his belief that the Father is greater than the Son and they are both different in substance (*homoiousius*), Arius and his faction attempted to garner votes for their side of the controversy. Unfortunately for Arius, he ran up against a very powerful man advocating the "one substance" point of view (*homoousios*). His name was Athanasius, later to become the Bishop of Alexandria. Some of our existing descriptions of Athanasius leave us with the unpleasant impression that he was an arrogant and contemptuous man. He favored the doctrine of "Jesus Christ is God" and—because of his powerful status—Athanasius was able to carry the day. And, like magic, men created the "Nicene Creed." This creed states that Christ and God are one and the same. On that day in the fourth century CE, Christ became God and God became Christ. It did not matter that there was no such declaration by Jesus Christ in any of the Gospels that would substantiate this claim. After he refused to acquiesce, Arius was immediately excommunicated and exiled. But many Christians remained unhappy with the adoption of the term *homoousios* because it did not appear in any scriptural writings, Old or New Testament. This was the first time that the early Church had delivered a definition of Jesus Christ by fiat, and the belief that Jesus Christ is God remains at the core for most all of modern Christendom. It does not matter that Jesus Christ never made such a statement.

And this tradition of convening councils, issuing edicts and defining orthodox doctrines for the Roman Church by its bishops and other members of the clergy would continue throughout the next few centuries. There were many aspects of Jesus Christ and His mission on earth yet to be defined by the wise men for the centuries to come. However, the Arian controversy did not go away and it survived for several more centuries with different emperors alternating between decreeing it a heresy and accepting it as Church orthodoxy. Christendom was, indeed, torn apart over a diphthong: homoousios versus homoiousius.

Arian Christianity was very popular in the early development of Christianity and it spread throughout the Roman Empire. It would also expand to outside the Roman Empire. In having God and Jesus Christ as two distinct entities—related but different—Arian Christianity had great appeal to a wide variety of people. It seems to have appealed to their common sense. For the people at this time—as is the case for the people in our time—it was exceedingly difficult to accept that God, the All-Powerful Divine Creator of all that we see, would come to earth so that He could die on a cross. When the so-called barbarians from Germania overthrew the Western Roman Empire in the fifth-century by sacking the eternal city of Rome, they came as Gothic tribes of Arian Christians. They had been converted earlier by the Arian Christian bishop to the Goths whose name was Ulfilas. The word barbarian was basically a term used by the Romans for any non-Roman person.

As future theological and Christological controversies would arise, the need for resolution would also arise and this resolution would be accomplished by convening these Ecumenical councils. And there seemed to be no end to these Christological disputes. These councils would be convened at various cities throughout the Eastern Roman Empire during the first six centuries of the Common Era. At these later councils, the emperor would preside and the tradition established at Nicaea would prevail: the majority would define the doctrine and the minority would be excommunicated and exiled. This arbitrary process was very much like high-stakes poker where fortunes or fame could be won or lost. In our journey through the early history of Christianity, the important issue for us is not about who won or who lost—who was and who was not in error. My hope is to reflect upon the arbitrary process of how *men* created the Christian creeds and doctrines that are now intrinsically a part of modern Christianity. With Roman Emperors presiding over these councils, and with the politics of power influencing the Church leaders who gathered at these councils to create Church doctrines—we have lost the essential truth in the message of Christ. Conspicuously missing at these councils was any mention about the fellowship of humanity or about love and compassion. The Greek term "agape" does not appear in any of the records from these councils. But we did get some Greek terms: homoousios and homoiousius.

It may also be noted that these early Ecumenical councils never really solved the nature of Jesus Christ or His relationship with God. The exact nature of the relationship between the Christ Spirit—the Spirit that dwelled within the man we know as Jesus of Nazareth—and God the Father is beyond our intellectual efforts to define with our words. What these councils accomplished was to make Jesus Christ a complicated and distant abstraction. He has become remote, and this remoteness renders Him without relevance for our times. When we attempt to delineate the ineffable nature of God with words and logic, we will *always* fail. These early Church leaders did, however, accomplish other political and institutional goals that would provide the Roman Church with the foundation it needed to conduct its policies and relationships with the emerging nations of Europe, but that result is beyond the scope of our journey.

The fourth-century Bishop of Poitiers, Saint Hilary, summed it up eloquently in his *De Trinitate*: "The error of others caused us to err in daring to embody in human terms truths which ought to be hidden in the silent veneration of the heart."

In addition to our discussion about the evolutionary process of creating Christian doctrines and creeds, we should now meet the Gnostics. Who were the Gnostics and why are these Christians so important to our discussion? They constituted the main and most important opposition to the early Roman Church—and the Church Fathers were keenly aware of the Gnostic movement, and how this movement was in direct competition with the orthodox Church. As we shall discover later in our journey, we can only imagine what modern Christianity might look like if some of these Gnostic beliefs had been integrated into Christianity. In reading the early history of the Roman Church, you will often see the term "Gnosticism" used to describe some of the early Christian heresies, and it remains a term in use by historians and theologians. However, this term, at best, is misleading and, at worst, it is meaningless. In *What is Gnosticism*, Karen King wrote about the problems in using the term "Gnosticism," by cogently indicating the problematical nature of this term. In *The Gnostic Discoveries*, Marvin Meyer wrote about this same problem of defining Gnosticism by referring to King's writing:

> How much more problematical, according to King, is the definition of "gnosticism," with rhetorical and ideological interests lurking at the very foundation of the term. From the times of the ancient heresiologists until today, King maintains, terms like "gnosticism" and "gnostic" have functioned as rhetorical constructs employed to designate the religion of those with whom one disagrees as "the other" and to name it "heresy."

The word Gnosticism has been used to include many diverse movements and some of these diverse Gnostic movements were often Christian Schools of Gnostic thought that could be completely antithetical to each other.

There was wide diversity among the Gnostic leaders during the first few centuries of Christianity. Such Gnostics notables as Valentinus,

Basilides, Carpocrates, Marcion, Cerdo, Marcus, Marcellina, and—considered by some to be the first Gnostic—Simon Magus exerted considerable influence on the early development of the Christian Church. But there were many diverse beliefs among these Gnostics. Many of these individuals founded their Christian Gnostic Churches based on their own ideas about the nature of Jesus Christ, and the spiritual purpose in His message. Similar to the leaders of the Roman Church, they had their own understanding about salvation, worship, cosmology and other religious concepts. According to Tertullian, the second-century theologian and heresiologist, the Christian Gnostic Valentinus was nearly voted Bishop of Rome (ancient equivalent to pope), but he ultimately lost support—and possibly this was our loss too. We can only imagine what Christianity might look like today with input from Valentinus. The Christian Gnostic Valentinians exerted a prodigious influence upon early Christendom and they went on to be one of the more viable alternatives to the early Roman Church. The Roman Church viewed the Christian Valentinians as their major competition and, therefore, they viewed them as their most dangerous competitor. Most scholars now agree that the Christian mystic Valentinus is most likely the author of *The Gospel of Truth*. This Gospel was found amongst the codices of the Nag Hammadi Library in 1945. We will explore more about this historic library later in our journey.

The Gospel of Truth takes the form of a beautiful sermon inviting us to experience the knowledge and love of God through Jesus Christ. Although this Gospel was very popular during the early years of Christianity, it never made it into the New Testament Canon. The second-century Church Father and heresiologist, Irenaeus of Lyon, vehemently attacked Valentinus and condemned his Christian Church as a heretical movement. The Valentinians—as well as other Christian Gnostics—were perceived as the greatest threat to the success of the early Roman Church. Many of the Church Fathers such as Irenaeus of Lyon, Hippolytus of Rome and the fourth century Bishop of Constantia, Ipiphanius dedicated prodigious amounts of energy to extirpate these rival factions of Christianity. After the Council of Nicaea, subsequent councils were convened to eradicate all vestiges of Valentinian Christianity, and any other forms of Gnosticism from

Church orthodoxy. With the omission of all Gnostic beliefs, we have lost the vibrancy that was intrinsic to the original Christian message of love. In addition, we lost important Christian material by the exclusion of many Christian Gospels that were extremely popular among the early Christians. These gospels would not make it into the New Testament Bible Canon. Miraculously, some of these early Christian Gospels such as the Gospel of Truth, the Gospel of Philip and the Gospel of Thomas have been recovered in the Nag Hammadi Library. Again, the canonical list of New Testament books was created as a function of increasing the authority of the Roman Church. Individuals such as Irenaeus, Athanasius and Jerome would define the orthodox Bible Canon and they would determine what was best for the future of the Great Church.

At this point in our journey, it is time to examine the subject of what constitutes orthodoxy and heresy. To accomplish this task, I return to a passage from Marvin Meyer's *The Gnostic Discoveries*:

> *What is the source of the authority of the "orthodox" texts in the canon of scripture? From a historical point of view, orthodoxy and heresy may be understood as rhetorical constructs, as Karen King states, fashioned in the arena of political debate. Understood in this light, orthodoxy and heresy have little to do with truth and falsehood and everything to do with power and position. In a vote, the majority defines what is orthodox, and the minority is charged with being heretical. Among competing political factions, the dominant force dictates what is orthodox; those less powerful are designated as heretical. And the winners define the Bible. Athanasius of all people should have been aware of the political and rhetorical aspects and implications of the discussion of orthodoxy, heresy, and canon. In the course of the fourth century, Athanasius was exiled as a heretic and recalled from exile as a champion of orthodoxy five times, depending on the latest vote of a council or the latest political move of a ruler. As a result, Athanasius spent much of the century packing and unpacking his luggage, until finally he was declared the victor in the battle for orthodoxy.*

> *Such are the issues that determine what sacred texts are considered authoritative and canonical—and orthodox.*

For our understanding of Gnosticism, I will try to distill—and, consequently, simplify—Gnosticism down to a few general points held in common among most of the Gnostic schools of thought. (For more knowledge about this subject, please see the bibliography.) "Gnostic" comes from the Greek word *gnosis* and is translated as our English word "knowledge." One of the themes most Gnostics have in common is the belief that by possessing a special type of spiritual knowledge (Gnosis), we will find salvation from our material existence. This spiritual knowledge is more akin to mystical revelation and, as such, it differs from academic or intellectual insight. Salvation is understood as the path to enlightenment—the path to truth. The path to salvation (enlightenment) begins with our understanding that a divine spark from God ("The One" or "Father of All") is contained within our material (physical) body. This divine spark is our human spirit, and it has come down from God to reside within our physical form from the kingdom of heaven, which is our true spiritual home. Our divine spark is an emanation from the fullness of God's divinity. According to the Gnostic view, our divine spark has become trapped in our material world. The Christian Gnostics believed that we need to always be wary of our place of entrapment, the material world. It is *not* our true home, and it is a place of great distraction, deception and degeneration. Our purpose, as trapped humanity, is to escape our material bonds and return to our "Father" and to the kingdom of heaven, our true home.

The knowledge (Gnosis) needed for our salvation is the truth that will set us free from our earthly bonds. As such, it is not the type of knowledge we garner from reading books such as in our intellectual or academic learning. This type of gnosis is a spiritual knowledge about our inner self and it is knowledge about the structure of the cosmos. According to the Christian Gnostic, this knowledge will be found in the message of Jesus Christ. The Christian Gnostic is seeking this knowledge by developing their direct intuition of Jesus Christ. The Christian Gnostic believed that the truth was in the message that Jesus Christ brought to earth, and it can be discovered through meditation, reflection and intuition. For the Gnostic, enlightenment is found within us, and there is no need to seek out middle-men to develop our inner enlightenment. We are to go within ourselves to discover the truth. In this inward search, we are reminded of the Socratic dictum: "Know thyself." The Gnostic is searching for the truth that lies within us. This kind of truth can be expressed in the concept of a Platonic form, which we already possess—but we need to reawaken this truth within us. Just like the Platonic form of truth and knowledge, Gnosis is the highest form of truth and knowledge. It is the form of truth that all other expressions of truth must participate in, if they are to be called truth. One of my most cherished elucidations about this type of knowledge or truth can be found in Plato's allegory of the "Cave." (So important to our journey that I have included it at the end of our journey)

By dwelling within the man called Jesus of Nazareth, the Christ Spirit was able to walk amongst us and teach us the spiritual truth that we need for our journey back to our spiritual home. His instructions to us were about finding God within ourselves and how we may be at one with our Father, the Creator of all creation. And by practicing the Christ message of love, we will learn how to love one another and how to live with each other. The Christian Gnostics recognized two forms of teaching by Jesus Christ. There were His teachings for the "common man" and there were His secret teachings for only His disciples. Jesus Christ, in the New Testament Gospels, refers to His secret teaching, and there is more revealed about this secret teaching in the Gospel of Thomas from the Nag Hammadi Library. The dual nature of Christ's teaching is made very clear in the canonical Gospel of Mark: "And with many such parables, He spoke the word to them as they were able to hear it. But without a parable, He did not speak to them. And when they were alone, He explained all things to His disciples." (Mark 4:33–34) The esoteric teaching of Jesus Christ, which the Gospel of Mark is referring to, discloses the spiritual knowledge the Gnostic is seeking. If we are not searching for this knowledge (Gnosis), we will be compelled by desires of the flesh.

This notion of searching for esoteric spiritual knowledge about God and about our true human nature is not new or unique to the Gnostics. Before the Gnostics, there were the Hermetic theosophists who were also seeking enlightenment by searching for spiritual revelation. Within the *Corpus Hermeticum*, an ancient group of Egyptian books written most likely between the first and second centuries, but based upon a much older tradition, there is a text entitled the *Poimandres*. And written in this text is the statement, "Ignorance of God is the greatest evil among men." (*Poimandres*, Treatise VII) We may understand this statement if we think about all the evil (ignorant) acts committed by people throughout our human history. These people, who were acting in ignorance of God, were able to perform their evil deeds because they were acting solely on behalf of their own rapacious self-interest. But if we possess *true* knowledge of God, as Jesus Christ taught, we will understand that God is our loving Father and we are His-Her children. God equals love. With our knowledge of God, we will always do our best to treat all of God's creation with our love. Merely professing our belief in God, without demonstrating love in all of our affairs, is tantamount to our ignorance of God. The people who have committed atrocities may tell us that they believed in God, but they were ignorant of God: knowing God is to know love and compassion for our fellow man and woman.

For the Hermetic theosophist and the Christian Gnostic, God is not simply the Father in heaven; he is also the God within us all. Our *true* knowledge of God will prevent us from committing evil (ignorant) acts. And knowledge of God is more than giving lip service to our belief in God: it is a commitment to practicing the love of God in all we do. When we develop love and compassion in all our relationships with our fellow man and women, we are actually transformed into Christ-like beings. While the Christian Gnostics enjoyed their practice of rituals such as the sacraments in their church liturgies, it was their search for spiritual knowledge (Gnosis) that was their first order of the day. In the Gospel of Thomas, found in the codices of the Nag Hammadi Library, Jesus Christ offers us these words: "I shall give you what no eye has seen, what no ear has heard, what no hand has touched, what has not arisen in the human heart" (Gospel of Thomas 17). The Gospel of Thomas goes on to tell us that, if we understand these words of Jesus Christ, we "will not taste death."

I will conclude this chapter with a few words about the Nag Hammadi Library. I find it exceedingly amazing that almost everyone, regardless of station in life, has heard about the discovery of the Dead Sea Scrolls. And, to be sure, the Dead Sea Scrolls are a very significant archeological find, especially with respect to Jewish history and the Jewish Bible. But every bit its equal in historical significance is the Nag Hammadi discovery, especially because this discovery adds to our understanding about the development of early Christianity, and these books provide us with an alternate definition of Christianity. And yet few are aware of this discovery. I can only wonder if there might be some sinister purpose skulking about somewhere in the dark to keep this knowledge hidden from us, especially when we consider the tortuous path that has been taken to get these books translated and published.

The Nag Hammadi Library is a collection of thirteen codices found in December 1945 by an Egyptian man with the unlikely name of Muhammad Ali. He found these codices in a jar that was buried in the Egyptian sands near a site named Nag Hammadi. The Nag Hammadi Library contains a collection of thirteen different codices, and these contain the copies of ancient books. Among these books are Christian Gospels such as the Gospel of Thomas, the Gospel of Truth and the Gospel of Philip. Also found in the Nag Hammadi Library are books based on Hermetic theosophy such as *The Discourse on the Eighth and Ninth*. Excerpts from Plato's *Republic* were also found within this most fascinating collection of books. Some of the Christian Gospels in the library have been dated back to the second century—and possibly as early as the first century. We know, for example, that second-century patristic theologians such as Irenaeus and Hippolytus referred to some of these books in their written arguments against heresy. This places some of the Nag Hammadi Christian Gospels—such as the Gospel of Thomas— into the same timeframe as when the canonical Gospels were being written. The Nag Hammadi books were translated, in most cases, from Greek into the Coptic language and they were subsequently buried sometime in the middle of the fourth century. These books were most likely in use by early Christian Pachomian monks. These ascetic monks, named for their founder Apa Pachomius, were living in Egypt at this time. One of their monasteries was very near to the village named Nag Hammadi.

An important question to ask ourselves is why these books were buried instead of being destroyed. These books were buried in the mid fourth century by the Pachomian monks. This burial was most likely in response to the thirty-ninth Festal Letter issued by Athanasius, the Bishop of Alexandria, in 367 CE. This letter listed the Christian books that he considered to be the only canonical books of Christian Scripture. He was laying down the law about the Christian books that could be read by the Christians who belonged to the Roman Church. Earlier attempts at establishing a canonical list had been made by Irenaeus as early as the second century, but the New Testament Canon, as proposed by Athanasius in his letter, was possibly the first list that included the twenty-seven books of the New Testament. In the fifth century, Saint Jerome selected these same twenty-seven books for his Latin translation of the Bible, the Catholic Vulgate. However, the monks, showing their great love for their cherished Christian Gospels, chose to bury these banned books instead of destroying them, possibly with the hope of recovering them at a future time. The proper method during these early times, as is the convention for our own times, would have been to burn these banned books, not to bury them.

With the discovery of the Nag Hammadi Library and other ancient texts such as the books contained in the Berlin Gnostic Codex, we now have additional historical and religious sources to help us answer the question that I asked at the beginning of this chapter: is Christianity true to the message of Jesus Christ? Elaine Pagels, author of *Beyond Belief: The Secret Gospel of Thomas*, wrote, "Research on the Nag Hammadi texts is having an incredible impact on our knowledge of early Christian history—it is virtually redefining it." Based upon our journey thus far, we may now discern how men created the Christian religion from a process of arbitrary judgments, which were largely predicated upon maintaining the sociopolitical stability and ecclesiastical authority of the Roman Church. The major portion of their doctrinal work was completed by the start of the seventh century of the Common Era. Church rules, creeds and doctrines were created for their ability to increase and enhance quantitative growth in church authority at the expense of qualitative improvement in the life of its members. Although, it should be noted, the clergy belonging to the Church hierarchy did quite nicely. For the early Church to survive amid a hostile and competitive environment, the founders believed they needed to establish their total control and complete authority over all other social and political institutions. And, in doing so, they lost the most essential element in the message of Jesus Christ: universal love and human compassion.

In creating the Christian religion, men were simply doing what they do best: acting on behalf of their own self-interests. For example, we see that certain Gnostic beliefs in the equality between males and females—both in and out of the church—were completely ignored by the early leaders of the Roman Church, which was rapidly developing into a patriarchic and hierarchic authority. Some of the early Christian Gnostic churches allowed women to become priests, participating in all the sacraments and performing all liturgical rites. In the Gospel of Mary, found in the Berlin Gnostic Codex, we discover that Mary of Magdala was given a very prominent position by Jesus Christ in His Ministry. The importance of Mary's role in the life of Jesus Christ is also illustrated in the canonical Gospels by their depiction of her as the first person, man or woman, who sees the Risen Christ after His crucifixion. These gospel depictions speak volumes about Mary's importance to Jesus Christ. Not only would the Roman Church ignore these facts about Mary, Pope Gregory the Great would negatively distort them in the early years of Church history. Pope Gregory was instrumental in erroneously depicting Mary Magdala as the female prostitute who is mentioned in another gospel passage. These two women are not the same individual—and the church has recently recanted its position on this matter, but the damage has already been done. In the history of Christianity, the examples of self-aggrandizing behavior by members of the clergy are far too numerous to list.

As we continue in our journey through the upcoming chapters, we will discover many possibilities and potentials in the message of Jesus Christ that were ignored or distorted, and we shall learn the reason why these possibilities were excluded from orthodox Christianity. We will explore the Christian Gospels, including the

Christian Gospels that did not make it into the New Testament Canon and we shall become seekers of knowledge (Gnosis). And, fortunately or unfortunately, depending on your point of view, we will discover how and why the message of love and compassion that Jesus Christ taught has been largely ignored throughout the early history of Christianity, and this situation continues today. We shall investigate the main causes that have lead to the failure of the Christian religion today and we will discover why we ended up with "churchianity" instead of Christianity. In His Gospel, Jesus Christ taught us about God's love and how we are to share this love with one another. His message was not about establishing ecclesiastical authority and worldly power. Power is the illusion projected by man and woman, but mostly men.

Into the World of Thought

HERMES: *Even so it is my son, when a man is born again; it is no longer a body of three dimensions that he perceives but the incorporeal.*

TAT: *Father, now that I see in mind [nous], I see myself to be the All. I am in heaven and in earth, in water and in air; I am in beasts and plants; I am a babe in the womb, and one that is not yet conceived, and one that has been born; I am present everywhere.*

HERMES: *Now, my son, you know what rebirth is.*

—Libellus XIII of the Corpus Hermeticum

Listen within yourself and look into the infinitude of Space and Time. There can be heard the songs of the Constellations, the voices of the Numbers, and the harmonies of the Spheres.

—Poimandres, Corpus Hermeticum

Throughout the ages, our world, both oriental and occidental, has seen some great teachers sharing essential wisdom with us. For example, there is Buddha's teaching for the East and, in the West, we have the teachings of Jesus Christ. While both of these great teachers have provided us with much needed wisdom, I am choosing to focus upon the western tradition, by exploring the message of love as expressed by Jesus Christ. Whatever we may think about the nature of Jesus Christ, we must first concede that the Gospels referred to Jesus Christ as a master teacher (rabbi). And He was teaching us about the wisdom of life. However, before we can arrive at an understanding of the wisdom, as manifested in the message of Christ, it will be necessary for us to have a brief discussion about the nature of our mind. First and foremost, it is with our minds that we are able to apprehend our world and everything we find in it. So that we may be able to discern the wisdom in the message of Christ, it will be critical for us to have a fundamental understanding of the instrument that performs our investigation of this wisdom. And this instrument is our mind.

How does our mind operate? When we observe the phenomenal world, our mind is at work imposing its structure and meaning upon the sensory data that we are collecting through our senses. Our mind both collects and organizes this information, giving us an internal image of the outside world. By utilizing our mental processes, we are able to find meaning and purpose in our world. Is the meaning of our world—which we internally construct from the input of stimuli coming from the external world—intrinsic to that outside world or is this meaning the result of a pre-existing internal design? And are we in possession of this internal design prior to any of our experiences of the world? Because we perceive the physical world by constructing our internal mental image based on the information received through our five senses, can we ever really be sure that we *know* "reality" outside of our minds? Or we may ask this question by using different wording: does the world have meaning if there is no mind to perceive this world? Additionally, are we born with a mind that is nothing more than a blank slate, a "tabula rasa," as natural science would have us believe? Or is our mind a proactive instrument that utilizes preexisting patterns or categories of thought, imposing its internal structure upon the physical world? These questions may boggle our mind, but enquiring minds want to know.

In our modern world, our mind has achieved miraculous advancements, especially in the field of modern science and technology. The institution of science has now supplanted the Church's authority, and science is in the vanguard for our modern world. This is particularly true when it comes to our physical sciences such as mathematics, astrophysics and cosmology. Our minds have plumbed the depths of our universe and, consequently, we have been able to create models for understanding our very complex universe. The Big Bang Theory has been exceedingly successful in understanding the beginning of our universe. Scientists have also scrutinized the extremely tiny world of subatomic particles. And they have created theories for how these subatomic particles interact with each other and how they interact with the forces that govern their behavior. In the subatomic world of electrons, protons, neutrinos and quarks, we have constructed the Theory of Quantum Mechanics. This is the strange world where bits of matter can actually exist in two places at once. Quantum Theory, with its Heisenberg's "principle of uncertainty," has taken on mystical overtones in its modern expression. It is, however, exceedingly encouraging knowing that science, by postulating the "principle of uncertainty," has now finally acknowledged the reality that the mind is capable of changing the nature and the structure of the object that is under observation. (Although it is a bit dated, *The Tao of Physics* by Fritjof Capra still offers an interesting interpretation of the mysticism found in modern physics.) Scientists are also, at this time, engaged in searching for a particle informally named "the god particle." This name has been given to the particle by the scientists who are engaged in this quest. Scientifically, this particle is called the "Higgs Boson" and it may lead us to a new understanding of how the mass of *all* particles is created. This literally means that we may be very near to understanding that magical moment when energy actually creates mass. I find it both fascinating and revealing that the term "god particle" has been chosen for this moment of scientific creation.

In our attempts to understand the Big Bang Theory, as the beginning of both time and space, scientists have augmented it with newer theories such as String Theory, which has now evolved into M-Theory (Membrane) with its eleven dimensions of space and time. These extra dimensions of space cannot be seen by us, not even the scientists who postulate their existence can see them. They are invisible to the human eye, but this theory predicts they must be there and the calculus verifies their existence. Scientists have measured the stars that make up the galaxies and they have deduced, from the speed of the revolving stars, that there is some strange and mysterious matter at work, but this matter has hitherto remained invisible to all our advanced scientific instruments. They call it "dark matter" for lack of a more precise name. And by measuring the speed that the galaxies are travelling as they move away from each other, scientists have also found another strange and inexplicable force at work. They call this force "dark energy," and it is stretching the very fabric of space-time, scattering the galaxies farther apart at an ever-increasing rate of speed. We do not know the nature of this force, but we can measure its results.

Albert Einstein reworked the seventeenth-century Newtonian theory of gravity and gave it a twentieth-century manifestation in his General Theory of Relativity. His General Theory of Relativity was published after he published his Special Theory of Relativity, which was released a few years earlier. His Special Theory of Relativity revolutionized our concept of time and matter (mass). His General Theory of Relativity gave us a completely radical view of gravity and space. Either one of these monumental publications, on their own accord, would have been a prodigious accomplishment for any one man. He was able to develop these remarkable insights by the use of his mind. In working out his complete Theory of Relativity, he did not utilize any tool or material that was not already available to anyone else, except for his unique mind. Yes, indeed, all of the foregoing achievements are extraordinary milestones in the last century of scientific development. And all of these accomplishments are due to the evolution of our mind and the resulting development of rational thought. It now seems as though we stand at an awe-inspiring zenith where almost anything is possible. It would seem the time is now right for us to make another leap, and this leap should be into the nature of human consciousness itself.

With science having gained such preeminence in the modern world, it now seems to be a good time to reevaluate the relationship between science and religion. During the Medieval Period, the Church had most of the power and exerted its tight control over society. Basically, the Church told us what and how to think. With the onset of the Age of Reason, this situation began to change. It would now be rational thought and intellectual development that would take center stage in the affairs of man. Thankfully, the Church's authority began to wane and science would begin its climb to preeminence.

Fortunately, or unfortunately, depending on your outlook, it now seems that science has replaced religion in our understanding of man's place in the universe. However, science and Christianity no longer need to be seen as antagonistic to each other. In fact, they actually complement one another. There are no valid reasons for preventing Charles Darwin and Christianity from coexisting—and we have no need to propose a substitute theory of evolution that will compete with the theory of Darwinian evolution. Science and Christianity easily come together in a higher form of truth, as in the truth taught by Jesus Christ. Because the truth of Jesus Christ has been obscured and buried under meaningless words, we will need to discover the real truth that allows us to integrate science and God. When the ardent supporter of Darwin's theory of evolution, Thomas Huxley, told Darwin that his theory would "kill God," he was referring to a God that had been narrowly defined by the orthodoxy of his day. This orthodox interpretation of God seems to be as true today as it was in Darwin's day.

The conflict between God and science is both contrived and unnecessary. The orthodoxy of lesser minds has created this artificial barrier between Christianity and science, and they have done so based upon their misunderstanding of the Christ message. Jesus Christ taught us that we are both spirit and form. Our form is our physical body. Jesus Christ sought, on many occasions, to teach us about our true nature, which is why He often spoke of spiritual worlds such as the kingdom of heaven where the spirit of God dwells. He also spoke about the physical world where our physical bodies reside. The duality of a spiritual world and a physical world is clearly demonstrated by Jesus Christ in His well-known Gospel saying, "Render to Caesar the things that are Caesar's and to God the things that are God's" (Mark 12:17). In this gospel passage, Jesus Christ is asserting that each person is both a physical body residing in the physical world and a human spirit residing in the world of spirit. And we have important duties to perform in each of these worlds.

Science and Christianity do not need to compete with each other. Science operates in the realm of the physical world. It investigates— as it rightly should—form, not spirit. We can learn a great deal about the material forms in our physical world from science. Darwinian evolution, with its "natural selection," has taught us a great amount of valuable information about physical bodies in our physical world. It is not a perfect theory and no biologist would assert that it is. But, most importantly, science does not pretend to teach us about the involution and evolution of the human spirit. For this kind of spiritual knowledge (Gnosis), we need to return to the message of Christ. The antagonism between Christianity and science mainly derives from earlier attempts by the Roman Church, such as in the case of Galileo, to own both the physical and the spiritual worlds and, consequently, they have now lost both worlds. If I may be so bold as to paraphrase the words of Jesus Christ from the New Testament, I would say, "Render onto science those things that are of the physical world and render onto God those things that are spiritual." And we need both of these worlds for our proper growth.

Most of the perceived conflict between religion and science is derived from a misunderstanding of the first book in the Jewish Bible. Unfortunately, when the early Roman Church established itself and included the Jewish Bible into their Christian Bible Canon, they did so based on their misunderstanding of the Book of Genesis. Most people today are still in a quandary when it comes to understanding this ancient book. We need to remember that the Old Testament is the foundation for a very ancient, noble and inspirational religion: the Jewish Faith. In contrast, Christianity should be based on the words of Jesus Christ. And these words are found in the Gospels of the New Testament and in the other Christian Gospels that were excluded from the Christian Bible Canon. By including the Old Testament into the Christian Bible, the early Church leaders were hoping to render their new religion viable to converts from Judaism. In Matthew's Gospel, we find Jesus expressing His views on this very issue: "Do not think that I came to destroy the Law or the Prophets. I did not come to destroy but to fulfill." (Matthew 5:17) The use of the word "fulfill" is the significant term, and His two commandments about loving God and loving one another supersede all the Jewish Law that had come before His appearance on earth. We need to remember the application of law without the spirit of love and compassion becomes the rule of tyranny.

In actuality, the Book of Genesis metaphorically instructs us about *two* accounts of creation—one of spirit and one of form. (See the Book of Genesis) This dual account of creation in the Book of Genesis has puzzled biblical scholars for many ages. In the ancient book of the Jewish *Zohar* it reads, "Woe to the man who sees in the Torah (the first five books of the Old Testament) only simple recitals and ordinary words." There is, indeed, nothing ordinary about the Book of Genesis. But there is one truth we can definitely know about the Book of Genesis: it was never written to be a scientific treatise about the creation of humanity and the universe. Like all great metaphysical books that provide us with spiritual knowledge, it was written in the language of allegory and metaphor. How is it possible that anyone would believe that you can actually explain the creation of the cosmos and humanity by God with mere words created by humans? It seems to me that the cosmologists, with their advanced technology and mathematics, have a better chance of capturing a useful interpretation of creation. We will, in greater depth, explore the enigmatic Book of Genesis later on in our journey.

The Book of Genesis tells us that we are created in the "image of God." This statement imparts that we have been created with the ability to achieve self-consciousness and this ability is a reflection of the "image of God." This statement also indicates that we have been created with a mind, in the image of God's mind, which is capable of rational thought and freedom of will. No other living animal on our earth has such cognitive capabilities as man. As long as we are aware of the limitations, science is good for our rational mind and it may add greatly to the quality of our life. Science, like any other tool, can be used for our good or it can be used to destroy us. This will depend on how we decide to use it. We may, with greater enjoyment, conduct our scientific investigations into the nature of the physical world by remembering that the physical world is just one of the many dimensions that are accessible to our mind. With the appropriate respect for what science is, and for what it is not, we may allow ourselves to utilize scientific thinking in our investigation into our mind and the nature of human consciousness. While science has provided us with many exciting and interesting insights about our physical world, it has been unable to adequately investigate the nature of human consciousness. Human consciousness is the absolute essence of what it means to be a human being. And only by investigating how our mind functions will we be able to yield insights about our human consciousness. To possess consciousness is a miracle of the first magnitude and it is our gift from a loving God. Think about it: the universe would exist without you and I existing, but, notwithstanding, here we are. God's consciousness, which we may characterize as absolute love, is continually sustaining our consciousness.

As we have seen, the mind is a very remarkable instrument. But what is the mind, how does it work and where is it located? According to the sciences such as anatomy, physiology and neurology, the mind is a collection of neurons found in the gray matter of that organ called the brain. Of course, this definition makes perfect sense when one considers that these are empirical sciences and, therefore, this is the *only* answer that can be rendered by their practitioners. However, this does not make it the correct answer. Regardless of the brain's complexity, complication and sophistication, I find it strange that we would believe that a lump of tissue would be capable of achieving self-awareness. The construction of the brain is, without doubt, one of the great evolutionary miracles of nature. But is it the seat of consciousness? To understand why science would see the mind and brain as the same instrument, we need to examine an underlying and fundamental construct in the scientific model of human consciousness. In a word, it is called "epiphenomenalism." This untenable supposition was a contribution made to modern science by such early scientific thinkers as Thomas Hobbs and Thomas Huxley. Simply defined, this doctrine states that human consciousness is merely the secondary phenomenon (epiphenomenon) of physiological processes and, as such, it has no power to affect these physiological processes. Again, this seems a natural assumption to make when your investigation is *only* concerned with the physical body. Clearly stated, this scientific tenet means that you are conscious only because you have a body and brain, and our resulting consciousness cannot affect the physiological processes of our body and brain. The body is primary and our consciousness is the secondary result. Anyone familiar with the research that Dr Raymond Moody has conducted with clinically dead people will have great difficulty with this scientific tenet. Anyone interested in his work with the clinically dead will find an article about Dr Moody in Wikipedia. Furthermore, any Buddhist monk would certainly be incredulous about the statement that consciousness cannot affect our physiological functions. Buddhist monks, and many others, have been able to change their heart rate, pulse rate, blood pressure and electrical brain waves by using their mind during meditation. Science has now confirmed the validity of this activity and they call it biofeedback therapy.

Could it be possible that the human being is more than only a physical body existing in a physical world? Certainly, the message about other transcendental worlds and different levels of consciousness has been taught by *all* the world's great philosophers and spiritual leaders, including Jesus Christ. Indeed, central to the message of Christ is that we need to be preparing ourselves for the "kingdom of heaven" and Jesus Christ specifically stated that this kingdom is "not of this earth." If we are seeking spiritual insights about the mind, we will need to look beyond the natural sciences. Long ago, in the dim and distant past, one could find teachers such as Pythagoras, Plato or Plotinus who could harmoniously blend the message of God with the message of science—but such a teacher is a rare exception today. Galileo believed that the two worlds of God and science were *not* mutually exclusive, but his scientific notions did not sit well with the Church of Rome and he was punished for his neoteric ideas. However, his punishment was not as severe as the punishment doled out to Giordano Bruno for mixing God with science: he was burned alive in Rome by the Catholic Church in 1600. It's very difficult to find any love in this action. We may correctly conclude that the Roman Church did not countenance any deviation from their doctrines.

We will need to turn our attention to the studies of psychology and philosophy if we are to glean any information about how the mind functions. As an undergraduate student majoring in psychology, I found it amusing that psychology, which is the science that studies the mind, is actually misnamed. The root word for psychology, which is "psyche," comes from Greek mythology. For the early Greeks, Psyche was the personification of the *soul* who took the form of a beautiful young girl. And we all know that psychology is not the study of the soul. In my humble opinion, a more accurate name would have been nousology, where "nous" is the Greek term for the mind or intellect. Notwithstanding this error, psychology—specifically the work of Carl G. Jung—will provide us with some important clues about our mind. Jung's concept of the mind is both complicated and very fascinating. I will attempt a very simple overview.

Jung conceptualized the human mind as consisting of several regions. And these regions possess different functions. Basically, Jung divided the mind into a conscious (ego) region and an unconscious region. Within the unconscious region of the mind, there are two forms of functioning: the personal unconscious and the collective unconscious. Both of these forms of functioning operate at the unconscious level. The personal unconscious is that part of our mind that contains our unconscious personal contents such as our memories, emotions and thoughts about our individual life. One of Jung's outstanding contributions to our understanding of the human mind was his concept of what he referred to as the "collective unconscious." The collective unconscious is that part of the mind that functions as a kind of repository where racial memories and ancestral images are stored. These ancestral images may consist of ancient patterns of thought that encompass or revolve around themes that pertain to the *entire* existence of human beings.

Jung postulated that we all share in our collective ancestral experiences and these memories are stored in the collective unconscious region of our mind. For example, we might find such emotional memories as the fear of darkness lurking in the deep recesses of the collective unconscious region of our mind. This fear lingers in our collective unconscious minds from a distant past when we, as a hunting-gathering people, experienced our greatest danger during the darkness of night. There are many such emotional vestiges that remain within our collective unconscious mind from our evolutionary past. Our minds, according to Jung, are more inclusive and richer in content than the brain of any single individual life. We may frequently dredge up mental patterns from our collective unconscious mind and be completely unaware of their origin. These unconscious mental patterns may be expressed in our dreams and myths. Jung viewed the manifestations of the collective unconscious mind to take the form of what he referred to as "archetypes." This basically means—when content from the collective unconscious mind enters into our conscious mind—this unconscious content is manifested in archetypal patterns. Archetypes may be viewed as recurring motifs or themes that have ancient origins. These archetypes may be consciously expressed by us in our myths, religious symbols, arts, music, allegorical stories of humanity, etc. The archetypal function of our collective unconscious mind may be viewed as a kind of organizing agent for human thought. We will also frequently see these archetypes as recurrent themes and symbols in our individual dreams. As manifested in our symbols, these underlying archetypes are always attached to some deeper and ancient unconscious meaning. The purpose in Jungian therapy is to find this meaning and understand how it relates to our personal life.

With our simplified version of Dr Jung's concept of the human mind, we may distill this overview even further. For the Jungian, the mind is seen as something more than the mere brain. In addition to the personal content, our mind contains information from our ancestral past that our brain would not be privy to. Jung stated, "The form of the world into which he is born is already inborn in him as a virtual image." Our scientific understanding reveals a brain that begins its creation at the moment of physical conception and it grows as an organ within the body during the young life of the individual. At the moment of death, it ceases to function any longer. This physical duration of our brain precludes it from having content that has originated at some distant time in our ancestral past. In understanding Jung's concept of our mind, we can see that our minds, at birth, possess a priori functions. In addition to the Jungian concept of the mind, we may also seek answers about how our mind operates from other models of human consciousness. These models will also include functions that are present in our mind prior to our individual experiences and, consequently, independent of these experiences. Fortunately, the discipline of philosophy includes some of our best thinking about human consciousness and it will provide us with some excellent models.

We may begin to think about our mind as Immanuel Kant, the eighteenth-century German transcendental philosopher, thought about the mind. He conceptualized the human mind as having what he termed "a priori categories." One might describe these a priori categories as predisposed methods of assimilating the input of sensory data coming from the outside world. These categories impose their order upon our sensory perceptions of the physical world. According to Kant, we are born with these mental predispositions. For example, time is one of these a priori categories we possess in our mind prior to our actual experience of time. With the beginning of our first thoughts, we are already ordering time by processing it as having a past, present and future. We do not need to teach the developing infant about how to order time: this process is an innate function of our mind. Another of these a priori categories is space. We intuitively understand space (dimensionality) at the earliest moments of sense perception. As Kant developed his philosophy of consciousness, he saw the human mind as having a predisposed structure, and this internal structure was responsible for creating the external world as we *know* it. His "Copernican Revolution" states that the world does not impose its structure upon our mind, but our mind imposes it structure upon the world.

Kant understood our rational thought to be mainly concerned with imposing order on our sensory perceptions of the physical world. He further postulated another form of reasoning that is inherent in the mind prior to our experience of the world. This form of reasoning transcends our rational thought. He called this transcendental form of thinking "pure reasoning," and its function is to lead us to a higher form of understanding such as we might find in our ontological understanding of human existence. This form of pure reasoning will also enable us to formulate thoughts about non-sensory realities such as the concept of God. Kant forcefully expressed his views about God, asserting that God is the "ideal of the supreme good." Therefore, he understood that God is the foundation for any discussion about morality.

One of the more interesting developments in Kant's philosophy was his concept of a "thing in itself." In Kant's view, we see the appearance of an object, any object, because our senses perceive the appearance of the object. We are only able to know the *appearance* of an object. What we cannot know is the actual object itself, the "thing in itself." For example, when we look at a flower, we can see its shape and color. We can also touch and smell it. This phenomenon, which we call a flower, is knowable because our senses allow our minds to know the appearance of the flower. But the actual flower in itself is unknowable. It is beyond our senses to know the actual flower that causes the appearance of the flower. Kant referred to the actual object, the "thing in itself," as the noumenon. This noumenon will cause us to see the appearance of the flower without revealing itself. While we can gain a rational understanding of the phenomenal world through the use of our senses, we cannot know the noumenal world because it is beyond our senses. It is as though there is a world out there that we cannot know with our rational minds. While we may, or may not, agree with Kant's thinking about an unknowable world, it is well worth our time to consider the limits of rational thinking. Certainly, any of the mystics or poets who have appeared throughout the ages would be familiar with the limits of rational thought.

In Kant's philosophy, as well as in Jung's psychology, we are beginning to understand the true nature of our mind and how it functions. When we are born our mind is not an empty vessel. On the contrary, we come into this world with a mind that contains preexisting functions, and it imposes its innate mental structure upon the world. Our mind collects and organizes the sensory data of experience according to its own internal structure and, then, it imposes this order on the world—unlike the conventional theory of perception that reverses this order. The world conforms to our mind rather than our mind conforming to the world. Contrary to popular belief, the mind is not a passive instrument—such as a camera—that simply perceives things as they appear in themselves. Our mind is a proactive instrument that is constantly imposing its own particular mental structure upon our physical world. Consequently, our mind is imposing its structure on the physical world, but it performs this function from outside the physical world. And this is the important concept for us to take forward as we continue on our journey. It is as though we are on the outside looking into our world.

Thusly, we may conclude that the mind is a metaphysical instrument and it cannot be put under a microscope. Because the mind is not a physical object, we are faced with certain epistemological limitations in our attempts to describe it. Let me try an analogy that I once read. In this analogy, we have a consummate piano player and she is playing a most beautiful piece of music on a finely tuned Steinway piano. The piano—a magnificent instrument with all the intricate details of its construction—is our brain in this analogy. The player—extremely superb in her abilities to create music on her piano—represents our mind. The music is the sublime and beautiful thoughts produced by the mind and brain as they work together. This is the wisdom expressed in the message of Christ. He is teaching us how we can create thoughts that embody the principle of unconditional love, the love God has for us. With the harmony created by our mind and brain working together, we may express the song of love, adding to the beauty of our world and glorifying the divinity of Christ. God's love is truly the celestial song that reverberates throughout our universe. It is the love of God that permeates every atom in the cosmos, imparting movement to all matter. God's love is the divine energy that sustains our universe and everything in it.

As Jesus taught, by using our minds, we can make a conscious choice to be either brutes or angels; to be hateful or to be compassionate; to be ignorant or to be wise. Our mind is currently the most powerful vehicle that we have in our possession. If we choose to clothe our thoughts with our base desires, we will live in a world of violence and decadence. If, on the other hand, we elevate our thoughts to express the love and compassion that Jesus Christ expressed, there would no longer be any selfishness, greed or violence in our world. If this sounds like heaven, that is because it is heaven. This is the kingdom of heaven that Jesus Christ is revealing to us in His message of love and this love is our path to truth. This kind of unselfish love is pure altruism and it leads directly to the development of universal brotherhood and sisterhood. The power of love is not to be thought of as an overly idealistic concept—nor is it an unobtainable dream. This concept of love is not for the frivolous minded. The love (agape) that Jesus Christ refers to in His Gospel of Truth is the power of God.

All we need to do is to earnestly and resolutely believe in the power of love, as taught in the message of Christ, and begin to practice this love in all our affairs. We will, then, manifest the love that Jesus of Nazareth is referring to in His Gospel of Truth. Jesus Christ clearly stated, "Most assuredly, I say to you, he who believes in Me, the works that I do he will do also; and greater works than these he will do, because I go to My Father" (John 14:12). We will incur failure by not believing in our ability to do great things. In the Gospel of Thomas, Jesus Christ tells us; "Rather the Father's kingdom is spread over the earth, but men do not see it." (Gospel of Thomas 113) By constructing our thoughts from the mind-stuff of love, we will begin to see the kingdom of heaven. This will be our new vision. If we truly believe in unconditional love, we will then begin to actualize our true potential and we will begin to live in peace with each other.

We have concluded, from our earlier discussion about the functioning of the mind, that the mind is not that organ in our skulls. We may now earnestly ask the question about the location of our mind. In attempting to answer this question, let us invoke the ancient Hermetic axiom, "As above, so below." These words are found on the *Tabula Smaragdina* and they are associated with the *Corpus Hermeticum*, a series of texts possibly written sometime around the first century of the Common Era. But the Hermetic theosophy expressed in these texts is much older. The Hermetic teaching has been ascribed to an ancient Egyptian hierophant (priest) living at or just before the time of Moses. Of the multiple names that have been ascribed to this mystagogue, Hermes Trismegistus (Thrice Greatest) is the most common expression for this mysterious sage. This Elder Brother's theosophy has emerged at various times throughout the last two thousand years, and its emergence has assisted in creating some of humanity's most significant periods of intellectual and spiritual growth such as the Florentine Renaissance in the fifteenth century. This fact becomes salient when looking at the work and life of Pico della Mirandola of Florence. Pico was so inspired by the Hermetic theosophy, which had been translated into Latin at Florence during his time, that he was inspired to write his magnum opus, *Dignity of Man*. Pico's writing, in its sublime depiction of man's potential, helps to inaugurate a new understanding of man's central role in

God's creation—an understanding that would be essential to the European Renaissance. We cannot over estimate the importance of putting man at the center of God's creation, and the effect this had on the renaissance of thought. This was the beginning of removing a religious institution from the center of man's experience.

In Hermetic theosophy, man is seen as a threefold being. He is composed of spirit, soul and body. In the Hermetic view, the cosmos is seen as being composed of a series of worlds, connected from the "lowest" physical world to the "highest" World of God—with the other worlds in between these two. Within this hierarchy of the cosmos, each world provides a vital function for man's physical and spiritual evolution. By ascending these worlds—from the "lowest" (physical) world to the "highest" World of God—we may come to *know* God. This ascension is our path to what Jesus Christ called the kingdom of heaven. It is our return journey to where we began, our spiritual home. The insight derived from the Hermetic axiom, "As above, so below," is an occult (hidden) truth explaining that the "lower" worlds are manifestations (or emanations) of the "highest" world, the World of God. The World of God existed before the creation of all the other worlds, and the "lower" worlds are fashioned in its likeness. When we read in the Book of Genesis that man was created in the image of God, we may understand that man is a spiritual reflection of the image of God—and the worlds where man dwells are also a reflection of God's dwelling place, the "highest" World of God. All worlds are manifestations of the one world, the World of God.

The primary mode of transportation in the physical world is our physical body. Likewise, the mind is our primary vehicle in the World of Thought. The World of Thought is the domain and *location* of our mind. The World of Thought may be envisioned as existing between our "lower" physical world where our physical body resides and the "higher" World of Spirit where our human spirit dwells. Although the World of Spirit is "above" the World of Thought, it is still "below" the World of God. Our human spirit, dwelling in the World of Spirit, is literally on the "outside" looking into the "lower" physical world through the prism of our mind, which is located in the World of Thought. A word of caution is advisable here. While we use such words as "outside," "lowest" and "highest" to conceptualize the cosmos, it would be more accurate to think of these worlds as existing within each other—a world within a world within a world and so on until we pass into the World of God, the kingdom of heaven and our true home.

According to the Hermetic cosmic structure, our minds may be understood to function somewhat like a glass lens, allowing our indwelling human spirit, which resides in the "higher" World of Spirit, to bring into *focus* our experience in the "lower" physical world. Our indwelling human spirit executes control over our physical body through the "lens" of our mind. Our mind controls our body by working through our brain. And it is our sacred duty to "polish" the lens, which is our mind, with the unconditional love we find expressed in the message of Christ. The mind that is filled with loving thoughts will allow our human spirit to quicken the movement of our physical body toward the wisdom of Christ. Jesus Christ is sharing this understanding of the mind, and of multiple worlds in His Gospel of Truth. This is why understanding our mind is so vital to understanding the truth of Jesus Christ. An example of Jesus Christ sharing His wisdom about multiple worlds in God's Creation is found in the Gospel of John: "In my Father's house are many rooms. If it were not so, would I have told you that I go to prepare a place for you?" (John 14:2). Also, in the Gospel of Thomas, we find Jesus Christ telling us, "This heaven will pass away, and the one above it will pass away." (Gospel of Thomas 11) Ultimately, all worlds will be re-absorbed back into the World of God.

From the aforementioned Hermetic account of our mind, we may discern some very practical methods for developing thoughts of love. By having unconditional love for our fellow man and woman at the core of our thinking, we will develop humane ethics and moral behavior. We shall remember that Jesus Christ taught us to follow only two commandments: love God and love one another. These commandments are at the core of the Christ message. It is not necessary for us to believe that Jesus Christ is God Almighty—although you may believe this if you wish to do so. We need only to deeply believe in His message of love, and that this love is our salvation. One of the most significant implications of this message of love, especially for our times, will be our ability to learn an attitude of compassion. No problem is too large or too complex to be solved if we approach it with compassion in our hearts. With love having primacy in our thoughts, we will begin to understand how to remove our ego from the center of our being. When we are able to empathize with the other person, no conflict will remain insoluble. God has given us mastery over our own destiny, but we need to open our minds to a new understanding of love (agape).

Because we have complete control over our mind and the attitude we develop, it will be critical for us to learn how to create an attitude that is conducive to learning about the spiritual love that *is* the wisdom of Christ. When I think about this kind of wisdom, I am reminded of what the Delphi Oracle told Socrates so long ago. Upon asking the Oracle about wisdom, Socrates was told that the wise man is wise because he knows that he does *not* know. This oracular answer, however arcane it may seem, is expressing a hidden truth. If we are to develop a willing attitude that will allow us to discern the truth in the message of Christ, we must first begin our journey with a completely open mind. We also need to realize that we know very little about the most important aspect of our existence: our spiritual dimension. The person who realizes his or her own ignorance has taken the first step toward knowledge. How else could we ever hope to discern who we are; where we come from; where we are going; what is our ultimate purpose in life? The individual whose mind has been inculcated with modern "wisdom," may recoil at such questions, believing them to be either nonsensical or to have no "real" answers. By adopting this attitude, his or her journey is stopped before it begins. Whereas the individual with an open mind—admitting they are *not* in possession of this important knowledge—has already begun their journey. This person is a Gnostic in the true sense of the word, and they are on the path to heaven.

Jesus Christ, again using His parables to share this wisdom, states, "Assuredly, I say to you, unless you are converted and become as little children, you will by no means enter the kingdom of heaven" (Matthew 18:3). Some Christian institutions would have us believe this statement should be understood as calling for the baptism of children. They are telling us that we must be baptized as children in order to enter the kingdom of heaven after our death. But only a Christian institution that is in the *business* of selling us salvation would have us believe Jesus Christ is exhorting us to undertake the sacramental ritual of baptism—administered by the authority of this *same* Christian institution. This is not what Jesus Christ is attempting to teach us. In this parable, Jesus Christ is sharing His understanding about a particular type of attitude. And this attitude is necessary if we are to understand His message. This attitude is all about love and acceptance. It is an unbiased and unprejudiced attitude such as we see in young children. This parable imparts a very important lesson for us: if we are to discover the hidden meaning in the message of Christ, we must first convert our mind into the open and trusting mind of a child. Jesus Christ is instructing us on how an attitude that is free from bias will allow us to understand His message, and this understanding will allow us to enter the kingdom of heaven. In His own words, He is not referring to a future time when we may enter the kingdom of heaven such as after our death. He is teaching us how we can enter the kingdom of heaven at the present time. The open and trusting mind that is filled with love is how we begin our spiritual journey, and this will lead us to our home, the kingdom of heaven. Our journey begins now. Conversely, the individual with a clever and sophisticated mind that remains closed may be in possession of a mind that is both dangerous to him or herself—and to others too. This is not the mind that will enter the kingdom of heaven. We should, as well, all be wary of Christian institutions that have a worldly agenda. Plato, in opposition to the Sophists of his time, crafted a most relevant and eloquent warning against such individuals and institutions: "Beware of shopkeepers with spiritual wares." This caveat is as apposite now as it was in Plato's time, some twenty-five hundred years ago.

A note to the seeker: In writing the preceding chapter, it has occurred to me that the reader may profit immensely from reading Plato's allegory entitled "The Cave." If you have not already done so, I sincerely urge everyone to read Plato's Cave. It has been included at the end of the book. I find this allegory by Plato to be a wonderful illustration about human knowledge, and it graphically depicts the different levels of human consciousness. Plato's Cave can also be found online at various websites and is available in Plato's dialogue,

The Republic. An allegorical account about human consciousness can often be the best method for circumventing the epistemological constraints that are present in all discussions about metaphysical realities. And Plato, being the master meta-physician, is able to do this with his unparalleled genius.

We have journeyed into the mind and through the world of thought. We have discovered the type of thinking that will make our world a better place to live in. If each of us would endeavor to bring unconditional love and compassion into all our relationships, we would begin to see marked improvement in all aspects of our lives and in our human institutions too. We may be well served to remember a line from a Beatles' song, *Strawberry Fields Forever*: "Living is easy with eyes closed, misunderstanding all you see..."

We may now continue our journey into the wisdom of Jesus Christ. This journey awaits us in the following chapters with a new understanding of the message of Jesus Christ.

Is Paradise Lost?

In every cry of every man,
In every infant's cry of fear,
In every voice, in every ban,
The mind-forged manacles I hear.

How the chimney-sweeper's cry
Every blackening church appalls,
And the hapless soldier's sigh
Runs in blood from palace-walls.

—William Blake

Love is a portion of the soul itself, and it is of the same nature as the
celestial breathing of the atmosphere of paradise.

—Victor Hugo

It is most revealing that we, as humanity, seem to have an inclination to project gloom and doom when thinking about our future. This kind of negativity has been translated into the modern axiom for our news broadcasting: "if it bleeds, it leads." If the story engenders our fear and abhorrence, it must be the lead-in story for capturing our attention. In looking at past generations, we will also see this same type of fear and negativity being expressed by our ancestors. And we continue to see this same projection of fear today. As we complete an end to a Mayan cycle of time and we begin a new cycle of time, we are again manifesting our fear. This is the same fear that was present at the end of the first millennium, and it was also palpable at the end of the second millennium. Amidst the people living at the end of the first millennium, there was considerable talk about the world possibly ending due to some apocalyptic event occurring. And, again, at the end of the second millennium, we heard a similar refrain being sung by the people. Computers were going to crash, causing planes to fall from the sky and, with computers failing, our modern way of life would certainly cease to exist. As we approach another re-cycling of time, which is coming up at the end of 2012 as foretold by the Mayan Long Count Calendar, we are again looking at the future with our fearful minds. What the Mayans are telling us is that one period of time is coming to an end and another time period is going to begin. It is not possible for us to infer—with any degree of certainty from either the Mayan calendar or any other extant Mayan writings—that this re-cycling of time indicates an end to our time by some event that will result in the total destruction of our world. Nonetheless, in our minds, this transition in time signifies some ominous and terrifying event coming our way. What if we, in looking toward the future, actually saw a wonderful and glorious event coming—some new vision that would allow us to see life in a different light?

Why we possess this intellectual proclivity for negative thinking has everything to do with our journey for spiritual knowledge (Gnosis). Our projection of fear is at the foundation of our existence in the material world and, consequently, it permeates most of our thinking. Fear is the demon that negates our faith. Our introduction to fear begins very early for us. Our parents and schools often use fear to induce the type of behavior that they desire in us. Our political and religious institutions are extremely adept at using fear to control us too. As children, we are taught that fear is the central theme in the Book of Genesis; fear of God; fear of Satan; fear of snakes; fear of ourselves because we are told we are born sinners. Instead of this negative portrayal of humanity—provided by those who offer us their exegesis of Genesis—we could be discerning the promise that is present in Genesis. John Milton understood this promise for humanity and he expressed it in his depiction of Adam and Eve in his *Paradise Lost*. It is the promise of freewill that allows us to make conscious decisions about how we will think and behave. Without this freewill, our consciousness would be similar to that of the animals, which do not possess free will. Having freewill makes humans unique among all creatures within nature. But, because of our fears, we tend to project the worst on unknown situations such as future events. We do this because we have been taught to do so. Fear is the last bastion for a weak mind. We peer into the unknown abyss and all we are able to see is our fear looking back at us. If we desire to fully explore our minds, we must embrace the freedom of thought that allows us to choose between seeing the future as something good (positive) or something evil (negative).

Although we possess the complete freedom to choose our thoughts, we have been trained to choose fearful thoughts. God has imbued us with our freewill at the time of our creation. In making our pilgrimage of descent into the physical world, we have continuously possessed a mind capable of freedom of thought. Our Father, who possesses perfect freedom of thought, has given us the same capacity for freedom of thought by creating us in His-Her image. Regrettably, we have allowed our minds to be manipulated by the purveyors of fear who lurk within our human creations such as our commercial, religious and political institutions. Without our conscious awareness, these institutions have been insidiously inculcating us with fear for most of our lives. We only need to turn on our nightly news broadcast or listen to the sermonizing by television evangelists to see how fear is being used to manipulate us. As we grow from childhood to adulthood, fear becomes increasingly pervasive in our lives, and much of this fear operates at an unconscious level. Therefore, we are frequently motivated to behave in ways that we do not understand. Fear is often the cause of our irrational behavior, giving rise to the most perplexing problems we experience in our world such as our intolerance, prejudice and hate. In our modern society, fear is so prevalent that we have learned how to accept it.

In our current state of affairs, we seem to have forgotten that we possess total and complete freedom of will, which includes our ability to choose how we will think about our human existence.

Understanding how our negative thinking prevents us from actualizing our potential is vital to our spiritual growth. If we are to *know* the good, we need to first think good (positive) thoughts and, consequently, we will do good (positive) deeds. We will need to remove the "mind-forged manacles" that are preventing us from having an attitude that allows us to see the truth. This is the power that our mind possesses in creating our attitude. Viktor Frankl sagaciously expresses this principle in his *Man's Search for Meaning*: "Everything can be taken from a man but one thing: the last of his freedoms—to choose one's attitude in any given set of circumstances, to choose one's own way." We must strive to develop an attitude that is free from fear and we will, consequently, unleash our imagination and creativity. Our freedom from fear will allow us to see and to value the divinity that resides within all living creatures. This is the attitude of love as expressed by Jesus Christ in His Gospel of Truth. By definition, an attitude of love cannot include fearful thoughts.

If we desired to create a religious institution, and our main objective is to establish its permanence from the beginning to the end of time, we would be hard-pressed to come up with a more advantageous belief than the concept of "Original Sin." Yes, a few men actually thought this one up early in the history of Christianity. This doctrine is not something that was taught by Jesus Christ, and it does not appear until many years after His death and resurrection. Among the first to formally introduce this concept was Bishop Irenaeus during the second century in his attacks against Gnosticism (See chapter 1). By creating the doctrine of "Original Sin," the early Church leaders could *not* have possibly found a more effective position to take for their cause. By declaring that all of humanity is born with sin, and their institution alone had the fix for sinful humanity, the early Church leaders were effectively ensuring their institution's permanence forever. According to this doctrine, we must become members and believers in the Church or else we will be doomed to spend eternity in hell. Eternal damnation serves as very strong motivation—and it utilizes our fear to maximal advantage. With their monopolistic stranglehold binding us to their commercial products, the leaders of our multinational corporations, such as the energy and financial companies, could still learn a thing or two about control from these early church founders.

The concept of "Original Sin" just might be the biggest hoax ever perpetrated upon humanity. You will *not* find this concept expressed in the words of Jesus Christ. As most of us know, this concept comes from an interpretation (or misinterpretation) of the first book of the Jewish Bible—the Book of Genesis. The Book of Genesis presents us with a very enigmatic story about man's beginning. This story was intended to be an allegorical work expressing hidden truths about humanity's beginning and about the beginning of our universe. The Book of Genesis was written in the language of mythology and it was never intended to be an open book that could be easily understood by anyone, regardless of their spiritual training. Because of their importance, again I add the words from the ancient book of the Jewish Zohar; "Woe to the man who sees in the Torah (the first five books of the Old Testament) only simple recitals and ordinary words." The Book of Genesis is to be read with great caution and with even greater spiritual understanding. Genesis contains information regarding our relationship with God and about our place in the cosmos. It is a book about how the divine spark from God was transformed into our human spirit, which animates our physical body by giving us God's "breath of life." The mysteries in Genesis can only be understood by the adept who possesses extensive spiritual training. In our attempts to understand the extraordinarily profound subjects, which are found in the Book of Genesis, we would need to possess the occult (hidden) keys to this text. Unfortunately, the early Church leaders were not in possession of the keys for understanding the wonderfully mystical account of creation found in the book of Genesis.

Any Jewish rabbi will readily explain to us that he sees no devil in the Garden of Eden. There is only a strange snake. It was centuries after the death of Jesus Christ when the Roman Church transformed the snake into Satan. In the book of Genesis, the depiction of Adam and Eve is to be understood as an allegorical description of prototypical man and woman who represent humanity at the time of our separation from God, and our subsequent departure from our spiritual home, the Garden of Eden. They are to be understood as the original *form* of man and woman, as in the depiction of "Adam

Kadmon" in the Jewish Cabala or as understood in the Gnostic concept of the original man known as "Anthropos." In representing the beginning of humanity, the story of Adam and Eve is about our emergence from our God-like condition and the beginning of our descent into the material world where we currently exist. This transition is reflected in the symbolic act of eating the fruit from the "Tree of Knowledge of Good and Evil." And this is one of the most important ideas in our spiritual journey to truth. For the very first time, humanity (early man and woman) made a conscious choice about how they will behave—and they made this choice based on their own freewill. We may view this as the first act of human volition. They possessed this freewill as a consequence of being created in the image of God. Adam and Eve, representing early humanity, utilized a God-given faculty, and we began to individuate from God as separate beings. Our separation from God is how we became self-conscious entities. And this separation is absolutely essential to our spiritual development. However, we are being instructed by our religious authorities the exercising of freewill—in order to gain knowledge about good and evil—was a sinful act. If exercising our freewill is a sin, why would God have given us the faculty of freewill? Did God create us without having a design for our future development? Without utilizing our freedom of choice (freewill), there is no spiritual growth. Without our spiritual growth, there is no reason to be a human being.

After making their conscious choice to seek the acquisition of the "Knowledge of Good and Evil," as depicted in the symbolic act of eating the fruit, Adam and Eve (early humanity) were *informed* about the consequences of such an action. Humanity was not cursed or punished for this behavior: they were simply *informed* about the consequences of their choice. As the story in Genesis continues, God is depicted as the voice that clearly imparts to Adam and Eve the consequences of their behavior such as they will now "know death." At this early time in our spiritual evolution, we were not experiencing death as we do now. Death, as we experience it now, is that period in between our successive incarnations. Early humanity did not have such interruptions in their stream of life. To "know death" is only one of the consequences that Adam and Eve (early humanity) were informed of—and all of these consequences are vital to the spiritual growth of humanity. By utilizing their freewill, Adam and Eve (early humanity) were made aware of the law of cause and effect. There is no curse in the story of Adam and Eve, as revealed in the Book of Genesis. Early humanity was simply learning a vital lesson. Maybe an analogy will help elucidate this point. If you choose to put your finger in a flame for a sufficient duration of time, I will tell you that your finger is going to burn. I will further tell you that it will blister and you are going to experience (know) pain. I am not cursing or punishing you. I am simply informing you of the consequences that will result from your action. And, by knowing pain, you most likely will not be putting your finger into the flame again. Pain is a blessing and without it you would continue to leave your finger in the fire until there was no finger left. Adam and Eve—symbols of early humanity— were experiencing spiritual growth as individual human beings, and this was according to God's grand design.

We are not "punished" *for* our sins (error); we are "punished" *by* our sins (error). In making their conscious choice to *know* both good and evil—and in their ability to choose one over the other—Adam and Eve (early humanity) manifested behavior that is essential for the spiritual growth of the human spirit. How can we ever expect to know the right path if we do not know about the wrong path? And if we have only the good available to us, how can we ever learn to become a better person? As the Greek philosopher Heraclitus taught some twenty-five hundred years ago, "There is no way up without a way down." We need to have choices in our life if we are to develop spiritually. Should we really consider the actions of Adam and Eve (early humanity) to be sinful? Maybe we would be better served by learning how to correctly execute our freewill so that we move toward the good (love) and away from the evil (hate). Each and every moment of each and every day is the time to be thinking about creating thoughts that allow us to implement Christ-like behavior in ourselves. And the message of Christ reveals to us the kind of thoughts that we need to create. Most importantly, we need to keep in mind His two commandments for us: love God and love one another. There is no greater love than the love expressed by Jesus of Nazareth by laying down his life for us. This is the expression of love we are to strive for in our daily lives. Yes, this sounds very difficult. Jesus Christ told us it would be a difficult task, but He also said we can do it. Why not take Him at his word?

Fundamental principles can be found in the truth of Jesus Christ—and these principles contain both practical and spiritual wisdom. This truth, if fully implemented in our daily lives, would literally create heaven on earth. In the Gospel of John, Jesus Christ states, "I am the way, the truth, and the life: no man comes to the Father, but by me" (John 14:6). In this gospel passage, He is telling us that He *knows* the truth—and it is this truth that will lead us to spiritual home, the kingdom of heaven where are Father dwells. Jesus Christ is not telling us that we must become members of a religious institution in order to find the Father. If we are able to learn the truth He is teaching us, we will, then, experience the kingdom of heaven, the abode of our Father. And the message of Christ is revealing the spiritual path to finding the truth—and it *is* this truth that is the *only* way to the Father. The message Jesus Christ delivers to humanity reveals God's truth, and this truth is love: love God and love one another. This truth is what He is referring to in the passage from the Gospel of John. As God's direct representative on earth, Christ is showing us that there is only one way to our spiritual salvation, and it is the path of love that will lead us to God. Christ represents God on earth, God represents love, and love represents the truth: love is our *only* path to heaven. No matter what name we use for our faith in unconditional love, it will be this faith that allows us to know the Father. Jesus Christ is disclosing the truth about how we can obtain our spiritual salvation. Jesus Christ personifies the love of God and it is this love that will lead us to our home, the kingdom of heaven. Jesus Christ, in the Gospel of Thomas says, "Those who seek should not stop seeking until they find. When they find, they will be disturbed. When they are disturbed, they will marvel, and will reign over all. [And after they have reigned they will rest]" (Gospel of Thomas 2). Jesus Christ is exhorting us to be seekers of the truth—to be Gnostics in search of spiritual knowledge (Gnosis). This truth is to be found in His message of love. It will not be found in the creeds or doctrines created by men. And Jesus Christ knew our Christian institutions would ignore and distort His message of love.

In His message, Jesus Christ is urging us to find the path to God's truth. Our path to this truth may lead us through the teachings of the Buddha, or through Lao Tzu, or through Plato. It does not matter which path you take—as long as you arrive at the ultimate truth that Jesus Christ is expressing in His Gospel of Truth. Absolute love is the nature of God and practicing this love in our lives is the truth according to the Gospel of Jesus Christ. This truth will be found in the message of Christ, and we will know that we have found this truth because we will, then, *know* the Father. In other words, we will have obtained the spiritual awareness of the kingdom of heaven. The truth, as expressed by Jesus Christ, is truly the wisdom of liberation: liberating love from hate; liberating spirit from matter; liberating humanity from ignorance; liberating good from evil; liberating joy from sadness; liberating health from sickness. Jesus Christ is offering us this glorious wisdom. And this truth will not be found in the doctrines and dogmas created by our Christian institutions. If we truly know that Jesus Christ is offering us this salvation, why would we ever desire to repudiate His gift? God's love is omnipresent—and we can participate in His love anytime we make a conscious effort to do so. To enjoy the love that Jesus Christ is teaching us, we need only make a conscious decision to accept God's love into our life and to practice this love in *all* we do. We will not find this kind of truth in any of the dogmatic assertions made by men.

Maybe we have lost sight of this offering by Jesus Christ or just maybe the Christ message has been hijacked by our Christian institutions with their worldly agenda. If we look around the world, it is not too difficult to discern that we are missing the message of love that Christ is teaching us—and we have been living without understanding this message for the last few thousand years. In the deepest meaning of the word, materialism is cutting humanity off from God. And this condition engenders our further separation from God. This unhealthy separation is the definition of hell. Hell is the complete absence of God, which is tantamount to the complete absence of love. In looking around our world today, we may be witnessing our own creation of hell. For example, can we see the presence of God in the countless wars that have punctuated the past few thousand years of history? Do we see God in the pervasive hunger and poverty that afflict far too many children in our world? Is God to be found in the hate and prejudice that galvanizes much of the behavior seen in the wicked deeds performed in the name of religion? Is God to be found in the violence that we inflict upon one another? Furthermore, is God to be found in the marketplaces of our Western democracies? The only god we shall certainly find in our marketplace is the god of greed. Greed, along with other expressions of self-centered behavior, is also at the root of the failure we see in our political institutions.

I think we can assert with confidence that something is amiss in a society where a person who *plays* a sporting game is richly rewarded with millions of dollars, but there appears to be no available money for our teachers in whom we entrust with our children's future. Our political leaders are also telling us that we can no longer afford healthcare for the aging, but there is *always* enough money for another war. And if these woes are not enough, we have dire ecological calamity awaiting us if we do not obviate the deleterious practice of plundering the earth with our insatiable appetite for the legal tender. Corporate pirates are putting humanity's fate in jeopardy, and we are drowning in a sea of consumerism. The major problem with capitalism is the capitalist, whose avarice has infused our entire economy with inequality. While corporate leaders practice their principles of unlimited profit, we are, at the same time, being told this is necessary to insure the stability of our free market economy. But, as we discover all too often, our economic system is anything but stable. As salaries for corporate leaders continue to increase at prodigious rates, the working man and woman have seen their salary remain flat or they have been laid-off due to corporate down-sizing. And with the further exploitation of third-world populations, corporate down-sizing will continue unabated throughout developed countries. Within our greedy desires are the seeds of our own destruction.

While far too many children throughout our world are living without adequate food and water, we are being told by the so-called conservative Christians that our free market system is compatible with the message of Jesus Christ. If these same conservative "Christians" would have been alive during the lifetime of Jesus of Nazareth, they would have defended the actions of the "money-changers" in the

Jewish Temple. They would have loudly proclaimed that such free market activity is our God-given right. The Gospel accounts of Jesus physically confronting the temple entrepreneurs is our *only* example of Jesus becoming physical with those He opposed. Therefore, this gospel story is providing us with a very important message. To fully understand this message, we need only to ask ourselves a few questions. If this free market activity was unfit for the temple of God, do we believe Jesus Christ would defend this same avaricious activity on Wall Street? What will history have to say about a society where the profit margin is valued above human life? Fortunately, Jesus Christ did provide us with the answer to our questions: "For what will it profit a man if he gains the whole world, and loses his own soul?" (Mark 8:36). As reasonable people, it is our right and duty to ask the difficult questions. Why is institutional Christianity failing to help us develop a compassionate method for living? Why are we failing ourselves? Where is the message of love and compassion that Jesus Christ taught?

One message is clear enough: we have not yet arrived at a full understanding of the message of love as expressed by Jesus Christ. We would be correct in asserting that true Christianity is yet to be understood or practiced on a large scale. We have not yet understood the words of our Christ—yet the beauty of His message is in its simplicity. The message of Christ is *not* a collection of abstruse doctrines and eschatological dogmas. The men who created our Christian institutions did so by creating their creeds and doctrines. Consequently, it is these Christian institutions that have obfuscated and complicated the message of Christ. It appears as though they were too busy with their worldly affairs and their power politics. The Great Church has endeavored to become "Rex Mundi" (King of the World) and all that remains is empty dogma. Our Christian institutions are failing us because they were not founded on the principle of love (agape) as expressed in the true Gospel of Jesus Christ. In teaching us how to begin our spiritual quest, the message of Christ is a simple truth, but its implementation will necessitate the retraining of our minds. The requirement to re-orient our mind reminds me of something I was once told while I was a member of a twelve-step program for recovery: "There will be some who are too smart to understand the message, but there is no one too dumb to understand it."

In a word, the Christ message is love. Jesus Christ gave us only two commandments to live by and they are all about this love. These commandments, if *fully* understood, and if **completely** implemented by us in our daily lives, will deliver nothing less than heaven on earth. We can find these commandments in the Gospel of Matthew. In this encounter, a lawyer attempted to test Jesus Christ. The Pharisee asked, "Teacher, which is the great commandment in the law?" Jesus Christ answered, "You shall love the Lord your God with all your heart, with all your soul, and with all your mind. This is the first and great commandment. And the second is like it: You shall love your neighbor as yourself. On these two commandments hang all the Law and the Prophets." (Matthew 22:36–40). Upon reading these commandments, we are instantly awed by their simplicity and profundity. No Hegelian dialectic is needed to understand the truth of Jesus Christ. All of Christianity should be based on nothing more than these two commandments. But do be aware: this is love (agape) in its deepest meaning. It will require our most ardent effort and our most devout faith to actualize the love as expressed in the message of Jesus Christ.

These two commandments reflect the truth at the foundation of the message of Christ. This truth is love—absolute and unconditional love. These commandments express the essence of Christianity as no creed or doctrine could ever hope to express. There are no problems on earth that these two commandments would not solve. In these commandments, Jesus Christ is referring to the highest expression of love. This concept of love may be understood in the Platonic form of love as envisioned by Plato, which is the perfect expression of love (agape). All other expression of love must participate in this form of perfect love to be called love. This is the love that Jesus Christ has for us. It is the love that God has for humanity—and it is the love that will save us from our ego-driven behavior. This love will transform our world into the kingdom of heaven. There is a song by Elton John, words by Leslie Duncan, named "Love Song," and it expresses this kind of love:

The words I have to say
May well be simple, but they're true
Until you give your love
There's nothing more that we can do
Love is the opening door
Love is what we came here for
No one could offer you more
Do you know what I mean?
Have your eyes really seen?
—Elton John, words by Leslie Duncan, Love Song,
Tumbleweed Connection

Who Was the Man From Galilee?

Hence when the way was lost there was virtue; when virtue was lost there was benevolence; when benevolence was lost there was rectitude; when rectitude was lost there were the rites. The rites are the wearing thin of loyalty and good faith.

—Lao Tzu, The Tao Te Ching

If the grandfather of the grandfather of Jesus had known what was hidden within him, he would have stood humble and awe-struck before his soul.

—Khalil Gibran

The most essential element in understanding the message of Christ is to understand the nature of Jesus Christ and how He knew the truth. In *The Heretics*, Walter Nigg writes, "Jesus Christ is the central question in all understanding of the Gospel." Unfortunately, words will fail us in this endeavor—as they failed the earlier bishops and patristic theologians in their attempts to precisely define Jesus Christ. However, I do believe that we can develop a very basic understanding of Jesus Christ. There are many among us who believe that a man, known to us as Jesus of Nazareth, lived some two thousand years ago, but we are not really sure who He was, or what His mission was. From the written historical record, such as the writings of first century Jewish historian Josephus and the first century Roman historian Tacitus, we do have proof of the historical man, Jesus of Nazareth. I think our time is here for an understanding of the spiritual meaning of Christ. He is a highly evolved divine spirit that chose to enter into our physical world for the spiritual salvation of humanity. This loving spirit came into our material world for one main purpose: to provide us with salvation from our physical condition, which beguiles us with all of its dangers of distraction and degeneration. The truth, as revealed by Jesus Christ, is showing us how we may return to our spiritual home. Jesus Christ is leading the way for us to return to the kingdom of heaven, our Father's abode and our true home. The historical Jesus of Nazareth was the human being in whom the divine spirit of Christ dwelled. Jesus had the physical vehicle that allowed the Christ Spirit to move about in our physical world. The Christ Spirit chose to dwell in the body of Jesus because, although he was human, Jesus was, and is, far ahead of humanity in his spiritual growth. He is a very special man. The Christ Spirit, however, comes from a much "higher" world than the world where our human spirit resides. We may accurately say His world is located at the "Throne of God" and this is why we can correctly say the Spirit of Christ is a divine spirit. Therefore, we can conclude that Jesus Christ was both a divine entity and a human being.

According to the Old and New Testaments, God has created a celestial hierarchy of heavenly beings such as the Seraphim, Archangels and Angels, to name only a few. As Christians, if we are going to accept the Old and New Testaments as the word of God, we must, then, accept God's creation of multiple divine entities, as depicted in both testaments. And it makes good sense that humanity would not be God's only creation. In fact, if we look at the original Hebrew word used in the Book of Genesis for God, we will find the Hebrew word "Elohim" is the word used to name God. This word, "Elohim" actually indicates plurality. Therefore, the first sentence of Genesis could be read as "In the beginning Gods created the heaven and the earth." My point here is twofold: first, from the time of the original five books of Moses, possibly written as early as the first millennium BCE, to our current translations of the Old Testament, much has been changed, rendering original meanings lost in the mist of time. Second, if we agree that God has created other divine spirits, which are unimaginably more spiritually evolved than humanity, why is it so difficult for us to understand that the Christ Spirit is one of these more advanced spiritual entities? It does not diminish the divinity or the importance of Jesus Christ to understand that Christ is not God the Father. In actuality, the importance of His mission to earth and His sacrifice for our salvation is increased infinitely in knowing this information: the highly evolved Christ Spirit accepted the request from His Father to enter into our physical world, and to become a humble servant for a lower order of beings. This is why His divinity is unquestionable, and His mission is the greatest gift ever given to humanity. With all our hearts and minds, we give thanks to this Great Spirit.

When dealing with such recondite metaphysics, as we do in our attempts to explicate the nature of Jesus Christ, we can do no better than to use the very same language that Jesus Christ used. Because His metaphor is directly understandable to our human mind, it will serve our purposes here. The expression utilized in the New Testament is the "Son of God." And, I hasten to add, until our minds have evolved sufficiently, this is as fitting an expression as we may find. Because we are human, we have no choice but to delineate the Christ Spirit in anthropomorphic terms, and Jesus Christ was aware of this reality. Using anthropomorphic terms will not constitute a problem—as long as we keep it utmost in our mind that we are doing so. At no time and at no place does Jesus Christ tell us explicitly that He is God the Father. He refers often to His Father throughout the Gospels, but nowhere does He say that He is the Father. He tells us that He will go to the Father. He shares with us that the Father is within Him and He is within the Father and, as such, they are *as* one. In the gospel of Mark, Jesus Christ refers to a secret that is known only by the Father: "No one knows about that day or hour, not even the angels in heaven, nor the Son, but only the Father. (Mark 13:32) In this passage, He is clearly differentiating Himself from God the Father. Jesus Christ also states that God is within man and man is within God. He imparts to us that the Father's abode is the kingdom of heaven, and it is to this kingdom that He will return. And, if we are able to apprehend the truth in the message of Christ, we shall also return to the kingdom of heaven. We could reasonably take the view that—if we are of a pantheistic inclination—allows us to assert that Christ *is* God, but, according to this same pantheistic view, we are God too, and so is everything in the universe—as well as the universe itself.

As usual, it was men who first deemed Christ to *be* God, and God to be Christ. This was done for several reasons. When the Christian Church was first given legal status by Emperor Constantine, it was confronted by many existing religious systems (See chapter 1). Many of these competing religions had very strong gods on whom they had been founded; this was especially true of Judaism. Orthodoxy mandated that the incipient Roman Church required a powerful God as their foundation too. But they were faced with a dilemma: their founder had been a humble man, a rabbi, who had walked, talked, loved and lived amongst the people. How was the early Roman Church to solve this problematic situation? The solution, as it turned out, would be easy enough for the Church leaders: they would, by edict, simply declare that Jesus Christ is God and it was God Himself that had walked, talked, loved, and lived amongst the people. The Church leaders further decreed that the woman named Mary actually gave birth to God, and God died on the cross. Incidentally, Mary and Joseph were the parents of Jesus the man. As we saw earlier in our journey, the "Christ is God" doctrine was mandated at the first ecumenical council in Nicaea and the Church leaders believed their problem was solved. Not only did the early Church leaders include the Jewish Bible into their Christian Bible, they also embraced the Jewish God as the Christian God. With the Nicene Creed, the Old Testament God became Jesus Christ and, along with the Holy Ghost, the Roman Church created their tripartite God. It appears to me that the ascetic poet-priest, Arius, had been nearer to the truth about Jesus Christ than the men who reviled him and branded him a heretic at the Nicene Council. (See Chapter 1) Due to the majority ruling at this council, we have lost the humanity of Jesus and the unconditional love of the Christ Spirit.

Although Christ is not God, the "Father of All" and the "First Cause of the Cosmos," His divinity is most worthy of *all* our adoration, devotion and love. And, because of His highly advanced spiritual evolution, His wisdom is our salvation. His truth will show us the path to our spiritual development and elevated awareness. Jesus Christ knew the truth as no mere mortal could have known it. He came to earth, on His own accord, to share with us the truth that comes directly from God. It may also be noted that He came here knowing that He would confront the ignorance and violence of men. He also knew His mission would bring Him great affliction and painful sacrifice. But still He came for us. His gift to us was motivated by the purest form of love. Without His brutal death and the subsequent resurrection, we would not be talking about the man from Galilee some two thousand years later. The story of Jesus Christ is the greatest story ever told and His love for us is eternal.

Jesus Christ foresaw that His message of love and faith would be completely misconstrued by men. As a divine being, the Christ Spirit possesses divine vision that allows Him to know the future. He knew what men would do with His message of love and compassion. He understood that men would fight over his message and shed blood over it, as no other cause has done. Countries and families would be set asunder in some of the most un-godliest religious wars in history. Massacres would be carried out in His name. He also knew that much of this bloodshed would be spilt by the same Christian institution that would make Him God. And Jesus Christ clearly articulates His understanding of what we would do with His message of love in one of the most misunderstood and most misinterpreted passages in the New Testament: "Do not think that I came to bring peace on earth. I did not come to bring peace but a sword. For I have come to 'set a man against his father, a daughter against her mother, and a daughter-in-law against her mother-in-law;' and a man's enemies will be those of his own household." (Matthew 10:34–36) We also find Jesus Christ giving us a similar admonition in the Gospel of Thomas: "Perhaps people think that I have come to cast peace on the world. They do not know that I have come to cast conflicts upon the earth: fire, sword, war. For there will be five in a house: there will be three against two and two against three, father against son and son against father, and they will stand alone." (Gospel of Thomas 16) Jesus Christ knew what men would do with His message of love and compassion, and these Gospel passages definitively attest to His advanced understanding of who we are. He knows the nature of our human mind, but, notwithstanding, His love for us is unconditional and undying.

Jesus Christ is the light and the way. And the really good news is that we do not need middle-men to have a relationship with our Christ. The Christ Spirit is within us and we are within the Christ Spirit. We need only to develop this conviction within our hearts. His mission to our world was to ensure our connection to our Father in heaven, and to provide us with instructions on how we may return to our rightful home, the kingdom of heaven. Christ has become our spiritual bridge to God. His gift to humanity is to be our spiritual shepherd forever. In the Gospel of Thomas, He tells us that He is "the light that is over all things." And He goes on to say, "Split a piece of wood; I am there. Lift up the stone, and you will find me there." (Gospel of Thomas 77) He is letting us know that, on our own accord, we can find Christ in whatever we do or wherever we look. But it must be each one of us, as individuals, that performs this search. Indeed, these are dangerous words to the Christian establishment. And it would not bode well for the future of the Great Church to have people hearing these words, which is certainly one of the reasons why the Gospel of Thomas was never included in the New Testament Bible Canon. With these words, Jesus Christ is teaching us to individually seek His wisdom about the love God has for humanity. He is not instructing us to place our faith in any man-made institution.

When Jesus Christ was asked about the nature of God, His response was to tell us that God is a "loving Father" and that we will find God within ourselves. Jesus Christ is all about God's love. Do we need an ecclesiastical institution instructing us in their lessons about where heaven is located or about how we must obey church doctrines in order to be allowed entrance into this heaven? We only need the Light of Jesus Christ to illuminate our path. He is our path to enlightened life. As we have seen, His two commandments for us are *all* about love. The love that Jesus Christ has for humanity was amply demonstrated by His very presence amongst us and by His great sacrifice. He continues to love us. And we can participate in His love on a daily basis. It is up to each one of us, as individuals, to seek the love of Christ, which is the love of God. Once we find this love, we will share this love with one another. His love is our path to the kingdom of heaven and we can begin our journey now. There is no need for us to wait until we pass from this earth.

To begin our search for the love expressed in the message of Jesus Christ, we begin with a change that comes from within us. It is an inside job. We will bring about an inner transformation that allows us to understand the message of Christ. If we are depending upon our social, religious or political institutions to effect these positive Christ-like changes in ourselves and in our society, we will be waiting forever. We, as individuals, must do the heavy lifting for ourselves. The greed that pervades Wall Street is the same greed that we carry within ourselves. The corruption that we see in our political institutions is the same corruption we carry within ourselves. We cannot expect man-made institutions to do for us what we cannot do for ourselves. We are responsible for our own spiritual development, and we will not need to rely on any institution for our salvation. If we arduously work on developing an attitude of love, we will begin to see the difference in our lives. These are *not* naïve observations about the potential power of God's love, and how this love can radically transform us. This is our spiritual transformation and this *is what* the message of Christ is all about. If we work on developing our love for God, our love for self and our love for one another, we will attract others who are also on this same journey. The overused expression, from eastern philosophy, is the term karma—but this is exactly what Jesus Christ is teaching us. Our love for each other is our most effective tool for breaking out of the greed and materialism that has shackled our spirit and imprisoned our soul. With the love of Christ, we can find the path that allows us to live in harmony with our brothers and sisters. We will soar high into the heavens upon the ethereal wings of love. Are we ready to begin this spiritual journey?

Love is a difficult concept to explain and it can be equally as difficult to perform. In our minds, we can see different expressions of love. There is the love parents have for their children; there is the love a man has for a women and the love a woman has for a man; there is the love between brother and sister. But, by far, the most sublime love is the love (agape) we have for God. This love is our greatest expression of unconditional love. This is the love that Jesus Christ was speaking about when He shared His message of love with us. Most of us have been taught how to love our family members from the moment we came into our family. As we grow, it seems as though our love for family is something that comes to us naturally. After we have children, we continue with our lessons about unconditional love. As parents, we try to love our children, regardless of their behavior. Since love is an attitude we can learn, we all have the potential to develop unconditional love for everyone, regardless of whom, or what, they may be. This is a daunting task, but, with our participation in the love of Jesus Christ, it is possible for us to achieve this goal. If we did not possess the capability of developing unconditional love for everyone, there would have been no reason for Jesus Christ to have suffered for us. I believe that a few words of caution may be appropriate to add here. In developing our love for all people, we do not need to endanger ourselves. If necessary, dangerous persons may be forgiven and loved at a distance. We may confront ignorance when we encounter it, as Jesus did, but we must always be mindful of the dangers in doing so. Our goal is to be the "peacemaker" by expressing our unconditional love for all of God's creation. This is the love manifested by Jesus Christ, who laid down His life for all humanity, including humanity's most ignorant and brutally cruel individuals. The life of Jesus Christ is our example of unconditional love.

Jesus Christ emphasized the importance of loving God and each other because this is how we evolve as spiritual beings. With our love for God and humanity, we fortify our own heart and mind. We do not love God because we hope to receive His-Her blessings. We are already experiencing God's blessings by being alive and conscious. Our unconditional love for God is the quality of love that we need to extend to all people (and all animals too). By learning how to develop unconditional love for God, we are learning how to love God's creation. And God's creation is humanity. The unconditional love Jesus expresses in His Gospel is the love Job had for his God, as described in the Jewish Bible. In loving God, we will love His-Her kingdom and all the creatures that exist within God's kingdom. If we are to regain our paradise, we will do so by preparing our minds to create thoughts of love and compassion. By eradicating fear from our minds, we will allow our minds to see a vision of heaven, and heaven is love made visible. Heaven is in our mind and we need to envision this paradise as existing here and now. We have the power to eliminate thoughts of negativity such as hate, prejudice and avarice by creating thoughts of empathy, love and compassion. Fear is the dark demon that spawns such negativity—and love is the glorious light that eradicates this darkness. God is the love we came here for, and the message of Christ is our path to God's love. No one could offer you more. Do you know what I mean? Have your eyes really seen?

This kind of unconditional love—as expressed by Jesus Christ—will only be possible when it is founded upon faith. This is the faith that we see expressed in the life of Jesus Christ. The development of faith can be a daunting task and the nearer to faith we come, the greater the temptations we will encounter. This danger is clearly illustrated in the New Testament story about Jesus Christ going into the desert and the temptations He confronts in the wilderness from an evil force. We are, as well, in the desert of materialism with a drought of love and our evil force is our fears. Our fears create the greed, hate and intolerance that separate us from the faith of Christ. By fearing our personal illusions of inadequacy and/or insufficiency, we become obsessed with the desire for more power and greater possessions. We, then, become contemptuous of anyone we perceive as getting in the way of our obsessive desires. And our obsessive desires allow us to justify the use of violence in pursuing our personal satisfaction. Viewed on a microcosmic scale, our obsessive behavior becomes the source of our own destruction. And seen on a macrocosmic scale, our misguided obsessions lead us into wars of destruction.

Our faith in the love of Jesus Christ and in His message will infuse us with complete confidence about our spiritual and physical well-being. We shall live with the knowledge that God is always providing us with all of our needs. There is no reason to fear inadequacy or insufficiency. This is the lesson that Jesus is teaching us in the Gospel of Mathew: "Therefore I tell you, do not worry about your life, what you will eat or drink; or about your body, what you will wear. Is not life more than food, and the body more than clothes? Look at the birds of the air; they do not sow or reap or store away in barns, and yet your heavenly Father feeds them. Are you not much more valuable than they? Can any one of you by worrying add a single hour to your life? (Matthew 6:25-27) These are not the words of religious doctrine or church dogma. These are the words of exalted liberation: forever liberating us from our fears.

Sadly, when our thoughts do turn to God, it is often for profit or self-satisfaction. Many people and most of our institutions, both public and private, have learned how to mine the mother lode of our fears such as our feelings of guilt. At its core, guilt is just another expression of fear. Guilt can be the fear we experience when we think we have done something wrong. Guilt can also arise when we fear something vital is missing from our life, and we believe it is our fault because we do not possess this vital possession. We anxiously await the next technological gadget as though these things will bring us salvation from our fears of insufficiency and insecurity. We are inundated with a deluge of commercialism—and corporations ensure our patronage by utilizing adroit methods of exploiting our human emotions. We need only to buy their products to experience feelings of happiness, love and security. Our politicians are commoditized by the use of slick and deceptive Madison Avenue advertising techniques—and these techniques often exploit our fears. Our politicians are sold to us as being great leaders of humanity. Once we elect these politicians, we are disappointed once again because we are unable to see any positive changes taking place in our society—only fear lingers on. Without faith and love, we are wandering lost in a material wasteland without our spiritual compass. And the message of love, as expressed by Christ, is our spiritual compass and His truth is our *only* way out of this madness. The truth He reveals to us includes the truth found in all other schools of wisdom. He has taken all the various versions of truth found throughout the world and He has distilled this truth into His two commandments: love God and love one another.

If we open our eyes and become fully awake, we will understand why violence is the only thing that is trickling down. And it has now trickled down to where we see it manifesting in our grade schools. The problem lies with us. Faith in love, as taught by Jesus Christ, is our only way out of our unfortunate condition. Our faith will lead to love, love leads to truth and truth leads us to God. On many occasions, Jesus Christ had to remind His Apostles about the power of faith. If faith was difficult for the disciples of Jesus Christ, who spent time in the presence of the Living Jesus, how much more difficult is it for us? We might do well to remember that the disciples were men and women very much like us. (Mary Magdalene was a devoted disciple of Jesus Christ and she performed a significant role in His ministry. See the canonical Bible Gospels for the importance of her role in the ministry of Christ and, for additional information, see the Gospel of Mary in the Berlin Codex.) Our faith may diminish from time to time, but the appearance of Jesus Christ in our world is God's proof that we have not been left behind without any hope of salvation. Most of us have probably heard the gospel parable about the faith of a mustard seed. This parable may sound simple, but it expresses a profound truth. The seed does not doubt that it will become a tree, it just *becomes* the tree. This is the faith found in the message of Christ—and this faith is the fountain that flows with love eternally. We need only to drink from it.

Our faith is the foundation upon which we build our love. Love paves our way to truth and truth is our bridge to God. The path of love will lead us to the kingdom of heaven. This love begins with us, and it will lead us to peace on earth. The truth is in the message of Christ and this truth can be found in the Gospels, including the Gospels that were excluded from the New Testament Bible Canon. I believe it is our time to read these wonderful accounts of Jesus Christ with our new understanding, our "new vision," if you like. We will have no need for institutional authority to interpret the words of Jesus Christ for our understanding. When we read these Gospels with an open mind and an attitude of love, we shall truly glean a spiritual treasure. We will listen to our heart for meaningful interpretation and we will use our head for a deeper understanding. The words of Jesus Christ no longer need to reverberate with the fear and damnation that has echoed from the pulpit for far too long.

With our new understanding, we will learn how to balance the rationality from our brain with the love from our heart. Our mind has made stunning advancements in science and technology (See Chapter 2), but our heart has been left behind. No matter the amount of material things we possess or how wonderful our material things are, we are left feeling as though something essential is missing from our lives. There is a hole in our being—and we have a deeply innate desire to fill it. But this is a spiritual need and it will never be sated by material possessions or worldly power. As the French mathematician and philosopher Blaise Pascal said, "The heart has reasons that reason cannot know."

We have split the atom; we have walked upon the moon; we have built the Large Hadron Collider in the hope of finding the "god particle." But, after thousands of years of civilization, we have not yet figured out how to live in peace with our neighbors. Jesus Christ shared with us the solution to our problems, but we have been unwilling or unable to learn from His message. In the formulation of our Christian theology, words of love and compassion were ignored. And with our rationalist sciences, man is now in danger of becoming a slave to the tyranny of his own abstractions. There are no valid reasons why science should be at odds with our spiritual quest. As we have seen, science deals strictly with the material matter in the physical world—and man exists in both the physical and spiritual worlds. We need to pursue knowledge in each of these worlds—always keeping in mind the purpose for each domain. We shall see that science and Christianity can, and should, complement each other. With the advent of our new understanding, we will see each of these pursuits integrated and we will witness humanity uniting the head with the heart. We will learn how to harmoniously combine love from our heart with reason from our mind, and the lion shall lay down with the lamb.

True Christianity is universal kinship—and we will find this harmony of humanity with our new understanding of love (agape). We may have a tendency to believe we are far removed from universal kinship, and such a reality is too idealistic. But this is exactly the kind of negative thinking that prevents the kinship of humanity from existing. Early in the seventeenth century, three pamphlets appeared in Europe that shared information about a new order of universal kinship. The pamphlets depicted a new way of thinking and living; a new community of brothers and sisters where love and compassion is the order of the day. These pamphlets excited the imagination of the people, and they had many Europeans talking about them. People were eager to join this new community, but no one could find them. The pamphlets, using the symbolic language of alchemy and concepts from Hermetic theosophy, expressed ideas about converting the base elements of humanity into the gold of spiritual awareness. These pamphlets were offering a new way of life, and it sounded heavenly, but, as people sought out this new community, it was nowhere to be found.

This universal kinship begins in our mind with our thoughts of love and compassion, and the people were not quite ready to apprehend this spiritual meaning. They sought this new community in buildings of brick and mortar. Soon the promise contained in these pamphlets splintered off into multiple directions, taking on different forms, and eventually returning to a state of dormancy. Maybe it was the people who slipped back into a state of dormancy. Positivism and rationalism were on the rise in Europe and the Cartesian "cogito" was taking center stage in the theater of the mind. Although it has been with us all this time, this universal kinship will have to await its rebirth. With our new understanding of Jesus Christ and His message of love, the opportunity for universal kinship will appear again. True Christianity will become a reality and, to ensure its rebirth, our task will be developing our faith and practicing our love. By creating thoughts of love and sharing this love with each other, we shall fulfill our destiny. As a song by the Eagles says, "It's a long road out of Eden," but our long and winding road will soon lead us back to our rightful home: the spiritual Garden of Eden. It is our journey and our choice. We can cling to our materialistic thinking and continue our time in the darkness of fear, or we can open our eyes and begin to see the light that shines from within the kingdom of heaven.

Are There Wars in Heaven?

Creed or Christ

No man loves God who hates his kind,
Who tramples on his brother's heart and soul;
Who seeks to shackle, cloud, or fog the mind
By fears of hell has not perceived our goal.

God-sent are all religions blest;
And Christ, the Way, the Truth, the Life,
To give the heavy laden rest
And peace from sorrow, sin, and strife.

Behold the Universal Spirit came
To all the churches, not to one alone;
On Pentecostal morn a tongue of flame
Round each apostle as a halo shone.

Since then, as vultures ravenous with greed,
We oft have battled for an empty name,
And sought by dogma, edict, cult, or creed,
To send each other to the quenchless flame.

Is Christ then twain? Was Cephas, Paul,
To save the world, nailed to the tree?
Then why divisions here at all?
Christ's love enfolds both you and me.

His pure sweet love is not confined
By creeds which segregate and raise a wall.
His love enfolds, embraces human kind.
No matter what ourselves or Him we call.

Then why not take Him at His word?
Why hold to creeds which tear apart?
But one thing matters, be it heard
That brother love fill every heart.

There's but one thing the world has need to know,
There's but one balm for all our human woe:
There's but one way that leads to heaven above
That way is human sympathy and love

—Max Heindel

In his essay, published in the early eighteenth century, Gottfried Leibniz coined the term theodicy. This term has come down into our time to generally mean the study of evil in a world created by an All-Good God. Our world was created by an All-Benevolent God, but we cannot deny the existence of evil in this world. How does one justify the presence of evil in a world created by an omnipotent and omniscient God? Theodicy is the vindication of God's justice. In their attempt to resolve the apparent contradiction between an All-Powerful God and the presence of evil, the early Roman Church rendered a very imaginative solution. As we saw in our earlier travels, the early Church leaders created the doctrine of "Original Sin," and, in so doing, they also developed a nefarious character—Satan—to account for the evil that we see in God's creation. These doctrines were eventually woven together to construct a rich and lively story about renegade angels who decided to wage war against God. It should come as no surprise that the patristic men of the early Church would project their violence and vanity into the realm of heaven. Certainly, this remarkable and mythological story is as imaginative as any of the mythology created by the early Sumerians, Egyptians and Greeks. Ironically, this story has a similar theme to the stories written by the Greeks about their gods on Mount Olympus. But, most importantly, it provided the early Church with its vital function of indispensability. Only the Church can save us from this theological catastrophe.

The Church's solution for the existence of evil is the story of an evil angel who became envious of God's power and jealous of man. The evil angel, named Satan, recruits a few rebel angels, declares war on God, and he and his legion are cast into Hell. This infamous character is, then, allowed by God to induce evil behavior in humanity (Adam and Eve), and he causes humanity to be thrown out of paradise. Due to the results of this heavenly war, and our consequent eviction from paradise, we are now condemned to live in a world where this evil angel will be allowed to practice his evil ways on us. In essence, this is what the Great Church calls "The Fall." This renegade angel caused Adam and Eve to commit the first sin. And, in addition to blaming Satan for causing Adam and Eve to sin, the creators of this myth also shifted the blame to the female Eve in this story. Although an All-Benevolent God created the world, evil will exist in our world because we are in a "fallen" state, and we now succumb to the influence of the evil one who reigns from hell. In the fourteenth century, Dante's *Divine Comedy* added the finishing strokes to this mythological masterpiece.

There is no doubt that we see evil in our world. But should we blame God for allowing a war to be waged in heaven? Should we blame the devil for this evil? If not, how do we explain the evil we see such as children dying by the millions in famine and poverty or the child who is born blind and/or crippled? Is this child afflicted with this evil condition because their father or mother, who gave birth to the child, committed sin? If this child is paying for humanity's earlier sins, as the doctrine of "Original Sin" would have us believe, how can we, then, believe in a Loving God? To pay for another person's sin would not be an equitable solution to our situation. The evil we see on earth such as wars, poverty, sickness, famine and greed are real. This evil must have a cause, but our Christian institutions are not offering us any logical explanations. They are offering us only their empty dogma and abstruse doctrines. And if we do not accept these doctrines, we will be known as non-believers, risking excommunication from the Church, and separation from our fellow Christians. If we are reasonable people, we are only left with the option of non-belief in God. If the truth was known, we would understand how man-made Christian theology has driven many reasonable people into atheism, and I think we can understand why this is so. Where are the answers to the existence of evil?

We know from our study of science that every effect has a cause and every cause has an effect. The law of cause and effect is an immutable law found in *every* study of nature. As we have seen in our earlier discussion, we are created in the image of God. This means we possess—as a reflection of God—a conscious mind that is capable of rational thought. Therefore, we should be able to find a rational explanation for the evil we see here on earth. Because we are rational beings, we will need a rational explanation of evil that passes the test of being a reasonable and logical solution. Did such a reasonable solution exist in the early days of Christianity? Did Jesus Christ give us a clue to the existence of evil? Was this solution eliminated because of political reasons?

It might be surprising to know that some of the most influential Christian thinkers, in the early days of Christianity, accepted the concept of the "transmigration of souls." This concept was expressed much earlier in Plato's philosophy, and it was also contemporaneous with the early development of Christianity, especially as borrowed from Neo-Platonism. Today we often refer to this concept as "reincarnation." The term, "reincarnation" is an extremely loaded term with many contradictory connotations, but we seem to be stuck with it. Incidentally, the term reminds me of some kind of a milk concoction, but I am probably dating myself with this comment. According to Plato and the early Christian thinkers, the concept of the transmigration of souls is the movement of our human spirit through its successive stages of development. As we travel on our spiritual pilgrimage, collecting our much needed spiritual experience, our human spirit needs to express itself by being reborn into different physical vehicles. Each new lifetime provides us with our necessary experience. And our multiple earthly incarnations will insure our spiritual development can continue unimpeded until we are ready for the next stage in our spiritual evolution. And, according to this concept, we always move forward in our progression, never backwards: as human beings we will always be human beings. There is no regression in nature.

According to the *Encyclopedia Britannica*, Origen (CE 185–254) was one of the most prominent, distinguished and influential theologians among the early Church Fathers. Even the celebrated Saint Jerome, who translated the Bible into the Latin Vulgate, which is still in current use by Roman Catholics, had great praise for Origen. For the first five hundred years of Christianity, Origen was one of the highest accepted authorities for the Roman Church, and his beliefs about the transmigration of souls (reincarnation) was readily accepted by many of the early Church Fathers, including such luminaries as Saint Augustine, Clement of Alexandria, Saint Gregory of Nyssa, Justin Martyr and Saint Jerome. Origen was renowned for his ability to syncretize the disparate threads of Christianity, including Gnosticism, into a splendid tapestry of Christian theology. Origen expressed his views on reincarnation very clearly in his writings:

> *If it can be shown that an incorporeal and reasonable being has life in itself independently of the body and that it is worse off in the body than out of it, then beyond a doubt bodies are only of secondary importance and arise from time to time to meet the varying conditions of reasonable creatures. Those who require bodies are clothed with them, and contrawise, when fallen souls have lifted themselves up to better things their bodies are once more annihilated. They are thus ever vanishing and ever reappearing."* (Origen, from A Select Library of the

> *Nicene and Post-Nicene Fathers of the Christian Church,*
> *P. Schaff and H. Wace editors)*

In *The Mystic Christ,* Ethan Walker writes, "In the first five hundred years of Christianity, reincarnation was most certainly on the main stage. It was a prominent and well-respected merchant in the bazaar of Christian theology." Sadly, as we have learned in our earlier journey, politics would again rear its contentious head. During the sixth century, Emperor Justinian opposed the concept of the transmigration of souls in favor of his "one life then heaven or hell" policy. It is speculated that Justinian thought this stringent policy would provide him with greater control over his empire. It is possible he was afraid of losing control over his kingdom if people accepted what appears to be a more lenient concept, the transmigration of souls, with its provision for multiple opportunities to learn our lessons. At any rate, to impose his belief on the Roman Church and his empire, Justinian called for a meeting of the entire Church in 553 CE. This meeting is known as the Fifth Ecumenical Council or the Second Council of Constantinople. While Origen was much respected and supported in the Roman West of the empire, the eastern area of the empire was more inclined to support Emperor Justinian. Justinian presided over this council, and the attendance was heavily weighted with the agreeable bishops from the eastern region of the empire. Unfortunately for Origen, the emperor was able to impose his will on the Church. Origen's views were extirpated from the Christian orthodoxy and he was deemed an anathema. Every since this council, the Great Church has pushed a "womb to tomb" doctrine of life. And the precept of "womb to tomb" existence has invaded almost all forms of current Christianity. In accepting Justinian's belief, Christianity has been the loser. We are left with no adequate answer or solution to why there is the existence of evil in our world. There remains only the Church's solution about some evil red demon running amok.

Because it harmonizes with the law of cause and effect, reincarnation appeals to the reasoning that is inherent in the human mind. It seems implausible to ask someone to believe that an All-Loving God provides us with the shortest of time—one human lifespan—and we, then, must pay for what we have done during this one short lifetime by possibly spending eternity in hell. And, during our one life, the devil is allowed to play hell with us too. This situation reminds me of demanding children to attend only one year of school, where they will be subjected to abuse by the meanest school bully, but insisting that they must learn sixteen years of education or else they will be separated from all humanity forever. Rationality should inform us of the error in this belief. If we are to learn the message of Christ about spiritual awareness, we are going to need more than one single life to understand all that God has in mind for us. We see this same cycle of rebirth all about us in nature. In spring, after a cold and dormant winter, nature's flowers bloom again. Humanity is a part of the nature of God and, as such, we also go through cycles of rebirth so that we may bloom again. This is humanity's inexorable movement toward perfection, and it is our path leading to God.

The really good news that Jesus Christ shares with us is about a loving Father-God and how this All-Benevolent God is providing us with multiple opportunities to learn our lessons. The more we learn about faith, compassion and love—and how we can extend this love to our fellow human beings—during our present lifetime, the greater our life will be in our next incarnation. We are on a journey to reawaken our spiritual awareness so that we may progress toward spiritually richer lives. Conversely, if we refuse to learn our lessons in our current life, we are compelled to repeat these lessons over and over until we learn them. Jesus Christ tells us in the Gospel of Mark: "Pay attention to what you hear: with the measure you use, it will be measured to you, and still more will be added to you." (Mark 4:24) In this passage, Jesus Christ is imparting the law of cause and effect. This is karma and no one escapes it. In this Gospel passage, Jesus Christ is giving us an important warning. If we see the child born with afflictions, we may understand they have some karmic debt to work out, but we *never* use this understanding as an excuse to treat such a child with indifference or disdain. We understand this child is afflicted because of some lessons he or she will need to learn. But our lesson is to *always* extend love and compassion—this is the message of Jesus Christ. And if we fail to help the child in need, we will incur our own negative karma, and our karmic debt will be increased because we failed to apply love when we had an opportunity to do so.

Reincarnation is not a reason to blame others for their unfortunate circumstances. We find Jesus Christ explaining the concept of the transmigration of souls to His disciples in one of the Christian Gnostic Gospels, the *Pistis Sophia* (Faith-Wisdom). He says, "Souls are poured from one into another of different kinds of bodies of the world." And what is the true meaning in the quotation attributed to Jesus Christ in the canonical Gospel of Saint John? "Except a man be born again, he cannot see the kingdom of heaven." (John 3:3) It is entirely reasonable that the meaning in this gospel passage is more profound than the orthodox interpretations that have been offered by those with the "born again" agenda. To say the least, the evangelical fundamentalist interpretation of "being reborn" is a very narrow and literal interpretation. Of course, we are told, by those who claim to have all the answers, that their assertion is the only correct interpretation. While their interpretation could possibly be *one* of the meanings intended by Jesus Christ, we will be well served to remember that He frequently offered explanations that expressed multiple levels of meaning. By utilizing this method, Jesus could deliver information to many people—who possessed varying degrees of understanding—and they would all receive the message according to their level of understanding. By having an open mind, we can be sure that we will not overlook His hidden meaning. And those with unreceptive minds will not hear this higher level of spiritual meaning.

I think we can safely assert that God is not responsible for the evil we see in the world. Man is responsible for this evil. When our ego is only concerned with our own base desires, we are acting as our own devil. If Lucifer exists, he exists within our mind. He *is* our base desires and our selfish motivations. We will manifest the devil in the evil deeds we commit. There couldn't possibly be a more malevolent spirit than the spirit of greed; the spirit of hate; the spirit of fear; the spirit of sickness; the spirit of violence. Within our minds, we consciously choose to allow these pernicious thoughts to grow into demons—and they begin to control our behavior. It is our beliefs that push us in the direction of our movement. Conversely, we may choose to eliminate this evil by developing our thoughts of love and compassion. These evil deeds only exist because we create them in our thoughts and, consequently, in our actions. When we are ignorant of love (God), we act solely in our own self-interest. Jesus Christ is teaching us how to rise above these negative thoughts in His message of love, and this is why He is our Savior. He will save us from ourselves. He is the Risen Christ and He is providing us with a solution to all the evil we see. The Christ Spirit is showing us how to create heaven on earth. He defeated evil and He is showing us how we too can defeat evil. In the Gospel of John, Jesus Christ states, "Then you will know the truth, and the truth will set you free." (John 8:32) and, because He is the Christ, He *knows* what He is talking about.

In the formation of all groups, by definition, there is something the sociologist calls the "normative function." Clearly stated, this "normative function" is the cohesive doctrines and beliefs that hold the group together. If a significant amount of its members deviate from these doctrines and beliefs, the group will disintegrate and, consequently, the group will cease to exist. The doctrines and beliefs that perform this normative function reveal more about the group or the institution that created them than they reveal about any truth itself. These beliefs are simply the cement holding the group or institution together. This is particularly true when it comes to our Christian institutions. In the previous pages of this work, we have seen how the history of Christianity has repeatedly revealed this fact to be true. With the creation of each new doctrine—and with each successive council—the Church was ensuring its cohesion and survival. This cohesion allowed the Great Church to establish greater degrees of political and social stability. And this stability has helped facilitate the development of authority that allows the Church to maintain its control over its members and over society as a whole. Unfortunately, these created doctrines did nothing to elucidate the spiritual message that Jesus Christ was sharing with us. On the contrary, they buried His message of love under the accumulation of abstractions.

When reading about the history of Christianity, one of the most important questions to ask ourselves is whether we have lost the essence in the message of Christ. And we need only to look honestly at our world to answer this question. We are in great need for real solutions to our current problems. The extreme examples of violence, hunger and greed we see in our world are symptoms that indicate we are moving in the wrong direction. If we are unwilling or unable to practice the true Christian message of hope, faith and love, we will find ourselves lost in a materialistic wasteland. We shall become adrift in a sea of pain and misery. If we are unable to bring love and compassion into all our human interactions, we will continue to see conditions getting worse here on earth. It is time for us to wake up. The alarms are sounding, and it is our time to heed the warnings.

The longer we defer our responsibilities, the more difficult our task will be. But it is not necessary for us to consider ourselves Christians. Our most important task is learning how to practice spiritual love for *all* humanity, as exemplified in the life of Jesus Christ. His life is our greatest example. We may even say that some of our greatest Christians were not actually Christians in name—such as the Buddha. Conversely, some of the most ignoble individuals are Christians in name only. This may sound like a paradox, but Jesus Christ is instructing us to participate in unconditional love no matter what we may call it. When our hearts are filled with love, and our minds respond to our hearts, we will always behave to the best of our ability. Love is our protection against our ego. Although many of our churches are failing to emphasize the message of love and compassion, we do not need to fail ourselves.

Christ is an eternal spirit and His truth is eternal. We need to understand Him as the divine spirit that He is, but we shall always remember that He is also a unique spirit to us—and for us. The Christ Spirit entered into the form of the man we know as Jesus of Nazareth. He walked among us and He suffered greatly for our gain. He gave this gift to us on His own accord and, at the same time, this gift reflects God's love for us. Because He lived among humanity, Jesus Christ possesses a unique insight into our human condition, and His message is designed specifically for our humanity. He is our personal Redeemer. The Christ message will redeem us from our self-centered ego. He understands what we are going through, and He has given us the spiritual road map to the kingdom of heaven. It is our task—by using prayer, meditation, and intuition—to commune directly with the Spirit of Christ. And we will find our Master within us. As the cave dwellers did in Plato's allegory about the cave, we need to release ourselves from the shackles that are binding us to the world of shadows. Our task is to escape the fetters of materialism, which are enslaving us to the physical world. We will, then, emerge into the bright Sun of Christ and our paths will be fully illuminated forever. There is no greater glory and there is no greater truth.

No Need To Fear the Reaper

To set up a hell in which God no longer has any say to all eternity, is to abolish the entire gospel. We must fight to the last breath, to the last drop of blood, so that the whole of heaven, the whole earth, the whole world of the dead, comes finally into the hands of Jesus. If we must abandon hope for a single man, for a single region, there remains an intolerable burden of death, a burden of woe, a burden of night and darkness, and in that case Jesus in not the light of the world.

—Christoph Blumhardt the Younger

You may call God love, you may call God goodness. But the best name for God is compassion.

—Meister Eckhart

Death must be ranked as one of the great mysteries on earth. When we pass out of this life, we go into the great unknown. And death awaits us all. As Jim Morrison of the Doors sang, "No one here gets out alive." And how true it is! Death is like the Sword of Damocles, always hanging over our heads by the thinnest of threads. But why should we fear death when it is as natural as our birth? The reality of death has taken on many different expressions in different cultures throughout history. The ancient Egyptian culture venerated death as a sacred journey into the afterlife, and this journey was essential if you were a great personage such as the pharaoh. In the Greco-Roman world, death became a journey into the dark place they called Hades. In the development of Christian theology, Hades became Hell and death would be defined by orthodox eschatological doctrines. These orthodox doctrines appear to be based, at least in principle, upon older religions such as the Egyptian story of Osiris and Isis. In Egyptian religion, the soul is to be judged after death as being either good or bad by Osiris and his judgment will determine your fate in the afterlife. As we have seen in the preceding chapters, this is pretty much the orthodox doctrine espoused by Emperor Justinian at the Second Council of Constantinople, and this became the doctrine accepted by the Church in the sixth century CE. However, this "one life then heaven or hell" doctrine does not appear in any of the recorded words expressed by Jesus Christ. Understanding death, as delineated by church doctrine, may give us a clue as to why death has become so fearsome. According to this orthodox doctrine, we live one life and, at the time of our death, we are confronted with an uncertain eternity. If we have made mistakes while we were alive, and we all have, we may face eternal damnation. If I believed this to be true, I would fear death too.

Death is an illusion and, as such, there are no valid reasons on earth or in heaven to fear it. I was about four years old when I first confronted death. A man from my neighborhood had a heart attack and died on my front lawn. I can still see him lying on the grass and I still recall the eerie and uncomfortable feelings that shook my mind and body. I did not understand what had happened, but it was the reactions of those around me that caused most of my consternation. My problem was there was *no* reaction or discussion about what had happened, and no one was behaving as though they had witnessed something out of the ordinary. The episode was completely ignored by those who were near to me. Only years later did I realize that those around me had no inclination to discuss this death because of the fear they were experiencing. Their own internal experience of fear prevented them from sharing their feelings about this event. This experience could have been a great learning opportunity, but it was overlooked due to fear. In my years as an adult, I have come to understand the power of fear, and how it has driven me to extreme behaviors. At the core of my emotional life, it was my fear of living that caused me to escape into an addictive lifestyle for many years.

Until I could confront my fears, my life was out of my control. I have come to understand that fear is one of our most deceptive emotions. Fear will often express itself as other emotions, but rarely are we able to identify it as fear. Fear is the devil that lies to us. Because of our acculturation, males—and possibly some females too—are reluctant to admit they are fearful. We have been taught to believe our experience of fear is a weakness. And this is why it is so difficult to deal with our own fear. Only in my later years did I realize that love, in its deepest meaning, is the answer. And love of self is how we begin to grow, both emotionally and spiritually. There is great courage and compassion to be found in those people with loving hearts. And Jesus Christ happens to be one of the great examples for us to learn from.

As we saw earlier on our journey, fear is the demon that will paralyze our minds and bodies. We have also seen how our religious and political institutions have, from time immemorial, used fear to control us. We, ourselves, will create fear within our own minds when we do not understand a person or a situation. Our fears about people from different cultures have created one of humanity's most enduring and vile legacies: racism. This immoral mindset made slavery possible. Among its many vile manifestations, fear also spawns the violence we see occurring throughout our human history such as our many wars. If we are afraid of our neighbors, we better dispatch them before they do it to us. Fear will prevent us from being the person we want to be. Ultimately, fear is based upon ignorance: ignorance of love, which is ignorance of God. If we *know* God is our loving Father, as Jesus Christ taught us, will we actually believe we are at risk from random events that are harmful to us? We find a wonderful illustration of this kind of love addressed in the Gospel of John: "There is no fear in love. But perfect love drives out fear, because fear has to do with punishment. The one who fears is not made perfect in love." (John 4:18)

Our society is rife with fears and these fears often reside within our unconscious mind. Because our fears are frequently unconscious, they will create our mental anxiety without us knowing why we are feeling anxious about our life. Maybe there are some amongst us who will only choose to do the morally right thing if they are motivated by fear. But, for those of us on this spiritual journey to find the truth, this is not what we are about. We desire liberation from our fears. If we are striving to live according to the truth of Jesus Christ, we will not need to fear anything, including death. In fact, we will actually welcome death because it is an indication that we are moving on in our journey to find the truth and, with our transition into the spiritual realms, we are getting nearer to our destination. The knowledge (Gnosis) we seek is the wisdom that Jesus Christ demonstrated for us as He walked on this earth. All four canonical Gospels, as well as the other Christian Gospels excluded from the orthodox canon, reveal that death was not the end to Jesus Christ. He conquered death, and he advised us that we can do the same things He did—and even greater things. (John 14:12) We need to take Him at His word.

By maintaining their dogma of eternal damnation, Christian institutions continue to exert their control over us. By having us believe that we are to pay eternally for the sins we commit during one lifetime, these Christian institutions have created a tyrannical god. This god has been derived from earlier religions by the men who formulated our Christian theology. This god is not the God of love, as expressed by Jesus Christ in His Gospel of Truth. Our future already exists *within* our mind: we will move in the direction of our beliefs and our thoughts. Our fears will move us into a perilous future. Fear is our most potent emotion and, as such, we will only conquer it with our thoughts of love and compassion, as expressed in the message of Christ. It is our time to turn away from our fear and negativity. We will be well served by recalling a quote by Gandhi: "A man is but the product of his thoughts. What he thinks, he becomes." Are we to be so thoughtless, as cattle in a herd, that we need fear to galvanize us into developing our moral behavior? Will fear help us to manifest our love and compassion? By all accounts, do we *really* need the fear that is imposed upon us by our many institutions? Is fear what it takes to motivate us in making morally sound decisions? After travelling this far on our spiritual journey, I think I know your answers to the foregoing questions. Conducting ourselves to do the moral deed is the reward in itself. Can we imagine a world where unconditional love would be the dominate action in all affairs, and compassion would carry the day? Imagine it.

Early in the history of Christianity, certain Church Fathers indicated they believed there were different degrees of understanding the Gospel of Jesus Christ. They made the assumption most Christians possessed a lesser degree of understanding, and they believed these individuals were unable to rise above this lower level of understanding. Saint Augustine wrote about two such levels of Christian understanding. Basically, he viewed the common man or woman—with his or her limited understanding of the Christian Gospel—as being fixated at the lower level of Christian understanding. He, then, went on to describe a higher level of understanding. At this higher level, individuals possessed a greater degree of understanding Christianity and the Gospels. Of course, Augustine viewed the church clergy as members in this class of higher understanding. The Gnostics also had a similar scheme for classifying Christians, but their scheme was more dynamic. Their scheme allowed for the movement of an individual from a lower to a higher level of gospel understanding. In their search for Gnosis, the Gnostic will find greater enlightenment as they advance in their search and, consequently, they will develop a greater understanding of the Gospel of Jesus Christ. As we read in an earlier Gospel quote by Jesus Christ, He spoke about the dissemination of esoteric and exoteric forms of His teachings. (Mark 4:33–34) This information, as imparted by Jesus Christ in the Gospel of Mark, may have been why Saint Augustine, and others, created their ideas about the different levels of Christian understanding. Unfortunately, Augustine, with his system of classifying Christians, introduced the notion of predestination into the theology of Christianity: some people will be touched by divinity, and they will receive the grace that permits them to understand the Gospel of Jesus Christ, while others will be unable to receive this grace.

The major problem with most of the classificatory schemes propounded by the early Church leaders, including Saint Augustine, is the underlying assumption of hopelessness: if one is born into the class of people with a lower level of understanding, they will most likely be arrested at this level without much hope for advancement. The Church viewed, and still does, most Christians as being arrested at the lower level of Christian understanding. At this lower level, according to the Church, we may find the halfhearted Christians who require the whip of fear to motivate their moral conduct. A whip, I may add, that still stings the spiritual flesh of the believer. In our spiritual journey, the important issue for us is to make a determination about the level of Christian understanding we desire to achieve, and how we are to achieve this level of understanding. We may, then, harmonize our new understanding with our actions. If we are seeking the truth in the message of Christ, do we really need an institutional authority assigning us to a lesser category of Christian understanding? Do we need fearful condemnation to motivate our spiritual growth? According to the truth in the message of Christ, we are seeking spiritual understanding because we are seeking our Father and the kingdom of heaven. We will be motivated by our thoughts of love and compassion. We may begin our journey with a limited understanding of the message of Christ, but our search for spiritual truth will allow us to ultimately achieve enlightenment. And all of this is possible through direct communion with the Christ Spirit. No intermediaries needed.

As we saw earlier, Origen, with his knowledge about the transmigration of souls, was a remarkable man. As an early Church Father, he clearly stood head and shoulders above the other bishops and patristic theologians of his time. He envisioned three categories of Christian scriptural understanding. The first was a literal (*somatiko*) understanding; the second was a moral (*psychikos*) understanding; the third was a mystic understanding. But Origen's real genius was to see men and women as progressing through these categories, from a lesser to a greater understanding of the Gospel of Truth. As we seek and find the truth of Jesus Christ, we are lifted up to higher spiritual understanding. We are not condemned to exist only at a lower level of Christian understanding. Origen believed we all have the ability to progress forward and upward into the light of truth, and so does Christ. Origen's understanding of the truth is full of human potential, and his beliefs displayed great love and compassion for humanity. But if these progressive ideas—and his assertions about reincarnation—were not enough to provoke the lesser minds of those who opposed him, his concept of apocatastasis would surely do the job. For Origen, this concept means that humanity, through our successive rebirths, will achieve perfection and, ultimately, we will be restored to God, our Father the Creator of All. According to the concept of apocatastasis, our goal is to ultimately achieve our perfection, which allows us to return to our place of origin, the kingdom of heaven. With his enlightened thinking, Origen effectively negated the Church's doctrine of death and eternal damnation—and he, therefore, removed all souls from existing in eternal hell. Origen was a champion in overcoming fear and he provided hope for the hopeless. When compared to the understanding evinced by his strident critics, Origen's apprehension of the message of Christ displays a much deeper understanding. Orthodox thinking is often the result of a lesser mind. With orthodox doctrines, no questions are allowed. Unfortunately, Origen was on a course to collide with the authority of his day, and he did so. As we saw earlier, at the Fifth Ecumenical Council, they pronounced him to be an anathema and condemned his work. Origen does, however, leave us with some words of comfort by advising us to be "inured to suffering and all misfortune, firmly armored by inner order and equilibrium, and finally blissful and like unto God in truth."

The wisdom of Jesus Christ is to be seen with spiritual eyes. This will be our new vision. On many occasions, Jesus Christ shared His understanding with us about the love God has for each and every one of us. He spoke of a forgiving God, a God that provides His-Her children with an abundance of opportunities to make it right. The God of Jesus Christ replaces the God of the Old Testament, and Jesus Christ replaces Mosaic Law with His commandments of love and compassion. Man is a spirit—a divine spark from God—and we are on a spiritual pilgrimage through the worlds, collecting necessary experience. And we shall return once again to our Father. Jesus Christ, as quoted in the *Pistis Sophia,* is revealing that our souls will have different bodies. Origen, the greatest of the Church Fathers, attempted to teach us about the advancement of our human spirit through progressive stages of spiritual growth. This is our spiritual ballet. We have no reason to fear death. What we see as death is only our human spirit outgrowing the usefulness of our physical body and discarding it. After discarding our physical form, we return to the World of Spirit to continue our work and, when the right karmic opportunity comes along, we are reborn again into a new physical body. Similar to every cycle in nature, we continue until perfection is achieved. This is the Wheel of Life, "Samsara," as seen in both Hinduism and Buddhism.

Jesus Christ, in referring to death and rebirth, employs one of His parables in the Gospel of John: "Most assuredly, I say to you, unless a grain of wheat falls into the ground and dies, it remains alone; but if it dies, it produces much grain." (John 12:24) Again, we need to understand the multiple levels of meaning in what Jesus Christ it telling us. What we call death is actually life: life moving through all of its various expressions. The truth—as seen in the message of Christ—is the path that leads us home to our Father. This is the path of love. It is *impossible* for fear, death, sickness, poverty, hate, greed and war to exist in a world where the love of Christ is diligently practiced by the inhabitants. It is our responsibility to develop our love—love for self, love for others and love for God. Compassion and love will transmute us and our world into a golden paragon of peace and serenity. This *is* the truth and this *is* the message of Christ. Just maybe the Christ message has been lost because it is so simple and so pure. There is no need to complicate His truth by creating abstract doctrines and nebulous creeds about Jesus Christ or His mission. These attempts to define the ineffable will invariably miss their mark. The creation of doctrines and creeds by our Christian institutions has only engendered disputation, division and bloodshed among humanity. Christianity should be *all* about unconditional love, and this will be the love that forms the foundation for universal kinship.

Our Homecoming

Let all the study of our heart be from now on to have our meditation
fixed wholly on the life of Christ, for His holy teachings are of more
virtue and strength than the words of all the angels and saints. And
he who through grace has the inner eye of his soul opened to the true
beholding of the Gospels of Christ will find in them hidden manna.

—Thomas a Kempis, The Imitation of Christ

This life is not merely what it seems to be. Hidden from our eyes by
the cloak of materiality is a wonderful world which only the eyes
of the dreamer can see and the soul of the mystic comprehend. The
stony walls of conventionalized thought and commercialized ideas
shut from view life's noble path. But as the ages pass, some see the
greatness of the Divine Plan and comprehend the glorious destiny
of the human soul. Sorrow, suffering, and loneliness are the great
builders of character. Man never becomes truly great until his heart
is broken. That is the supreme test. Those who are deepened and
broadened by their experience rise triumphant from the ruins of
their dreams and pass on to fuller destiny.

—Manly P. Hall, The Ways of the Lonely Ones

For those of us on this journey, there can be nothing more blissful
than our homecoming. As seekers of truth, our hearts yearn for
returning to our home, the kingdom of heaven. We have traveled far
and wide to obtain wisdom, always hoping that our home will be
found. It is, indeed, a daunting task to be in search of that island of

peace and serenity surrounded by a sea of confusion and nihilism. Without a doubt, it is a very dangerous journey. In our modern age, nihilism has become the new heresy. In our earlier journey through the history of the Roman Church, we saw how the theologians struck down the so-called heretics. And we saw how these heretics were often men and women of belief, faith and a deep understanding of Jesus Christ. Their only misfortune appears to be in the depth of their thinking and in the measure of their devoutness. Fortunately, today the Great Church has lost all of its power to burn a man or a woman alive for having variations in beliefs, and the spiritual heretic has disappeared. In their place, we have a new and truly insidious type of heretic. This new heretic is a nihilist and they are a much greater threat to us than any of the heretics from the past. The real danger in nihilism is that it is a "nothing" and you cannot confront or oppose a "nothing."

With the failure of Christianity in the Western World, nihilism has effectively permeated most of our society. We see it everywhere. Nihilism is at the root of materialism. Without beliefs concerning transcendental realities, people are looking to physical possessions for their comfort. Many people today believe metaphysical philosophies, including religious theosophies, are useless or they believe these ideas have served their purpose and they are now nothing more than moribund precepts belonging to an earlier age. In *The Heretics,* Walter Nigg writes, "Nihilism is a modern mutation of the medieval plague: spiritually, as many are dying of it as perished from the Black Death." No reasonable person could look at the world today and believe that we are on the right path. With almost half the children of the world living without adequate food and drinking water, surely we are missing something that is vital to our growth and well-being. In the affluent country of America, twenty percent of the children live below the poverty line. While there are those who possess great wealth, there is no excuse for us to allow children to suffer from hunger and insufficiency. When capital profit becomes more important than human life, it does not seem like an exaggeration to make the statement that we are spiritually dying. There must be a better way to make a living without killing ourselves. And there is!

Today it appears that the main sources of information for most people are, at best, found in the corporate owned television news outlets or, at worst, in the latest political or commercial platitudes. Slogans and "sound bites" parade as facts and our news outlets, which are owned by the multi-national corporations, are shaping our perception of the world. Political disputation has supplanted theological disputation. Many of our public institutions are rife with greed and corruption. And these problems are only going to increase as we further justify the economic principle of excessive profit over the value of human life. We are now seeing the consequences of an economy that is founded upon unlimited capital profit. We are, indeed, reaping the results of a system that is out of control. We may deny the reality of global climate change, but—like the alcoholic who is in denial—this behavior is currently catching up with us too. In the message of love, as expressed in the Gospel of Jesus Christ, there are ample instructions for converting us into better stewards of our earth. When we love God as Christ has instructed us to do, we will love His-Her creation, and we will demonstrate our loving care for the earth.

Just as in times of old, there are still certain individuals among us who call themselves Christians, and they will use the Bible to justify their condemnation of anything that varies from their belief system. In America, the term "evangelicals" has been employed to describe some of these self-appointed arbiters of morality. Although they claim to base their religion on the Gospels of the New Testament, they are actually ignoring *every* word uttered by Jesus Christ. These "evangelicals" judge and condemn every type of lifestyle that they do not understand. And, in their hubris, they claim they are doing so based on the words of Jesus Christ. Nothing could be further from the truth. We can find this issued being discussed in the Gospel of Matthew: "For God did not send his Son into the world to condemn the world, but to save the world through him." (Matthew 3:17) As our journey has hopefully revealed to us, Jesus Christ did *not* condemn anybody. His message and *every* word that is attributed to Him, in both canonical and non-canonical sources, is *all* about love: loving God and loving each other. By corrupting the message of Christ, these individuals are obscuring His message of love (agape), and, even worse, they are preventing many of us from learning His lessons about compassion and forgiveness. It is these distortions that are turning people against the words of Jesus Christ. And it is, without doubt, this kind of hypocrisy that is certainly one of the reasons why our Christian institutions are failing to share the word of Christian love. Intolerance and hypocrisy will not engender our desire to become a believer in Christianity. Where is the message about love? In looking at our current times, we are inexorably forced to agree with the lament made by Saint John of the Cross when he so eloquently expressed his thoughts of sadness: this is, indeed, "the dark night of the soul."

As we seek the truth in the message of Jesus Christ, how will we navigate the treacherous waters of deception and duplicity? How will we find our way back to our spiritual home? When we attempt to express our discussion in Christian terms, we will inevitably confront the insipidity these religious terms now represent. In our modern society, Christian words have lost their spiritual meaning. Our ears are filled with the hollow echoes of church dogma, and their hypocrisy is turning us off to spiritual exploration. In our everyday life, we feel as though we are far removed from the love of God and the truth of Christ. We find it exceedingly difficult to refute Nietzsche's statement "God is dead." But as intrepid souls looking to return to our home, like Homer's Odysseus, we will persist in our spiritual journey. We need to keep our faith in God's love for us, and persevere in our search for the truth about our life. We shall celebrate our search with the words from a Crosby, Stills, Nash and Young song: "Carry on, love is coming; Love is coming to us all." When it appears that life has become hopeless, we shall remember that, in times such as these, we will urgently need to find strength in the truth of Jesus Christ. During difficult times, I often remind myself of the words expressed by the ninetieth century transcendentalist philosopher and author Ralph Waldo Emerson: "Character is built on the debris of our despair."

Our attitude of faith and love will be the beginning to finding the solutions to our problems. And we can learn to develop our faith by looking at the life of Jesus Christ. He offered us one of the greatest examples of faith in all of human history. Throughout most of our history, the world has been a very dangerous place for those who practiced their faith. The expression of faith could literally be a life or death situation. But Jesus Christ never wavered in His faith as He stood before the high priests of the Sanhedrin, and was condemned to death by Caiaphas for the crime of blasphemy. His faith was equally evident as He stood before Pontius Pilate, and was legally sentenced to death by crucifixion. The very people he was born amongst turned against Him, and yet His dying words were to ask God to forgive them. This kind of love and faith can *only* be founded on the absolute knowledge of the truth—the truth as revealed to Jesus Christ by God Almighty. We need to understand that the Christ Spirit knew the will of God as no human could know. Jesus Christ is our brightest beacon, and His love will illuminate our path. His life and His message of love is humanity's greatest hope. He is our example to follow. The love that Christ is sharing with us will not be found in the arid doctrines of our Christian institutions. It will not be found in a locked vault located in some grand and stylish building. This love is not evinced by those who practice hypocrisy and intolerance. If we are willing to search deeply within ourselves, we will find this unconditional love in our hearts. Jesus Christ has vouchsafed His love and truth to us by his supreme sacrifice.

In actuality, we do not need to refute Nietzsche's statement about God being dead because the meaning behind this statement was, and is, true. Nietzsche is expressing the concept of a traditional and orthodox God that is no longer relevant to our time. This statement refers to the death of an anthropomorphic god who was conceptualized as possessing, among his many other human characteristics, both a vindictive and vengeful temperament. This is a concept of God as Nietzsche saw God depicted in the Old Testament. The Old Testament concept of God was certainly needed for a wandering people in a land of terrific violence and intense hostility. These nomadic people required a fierce God that commanded them to take an "eye for an eye." It was the Old Testament God who commanded Joshua, during his assault on Jericho, to slay all inhabitants of the city, including all women and children. This Old Testament God was a God of Jewish Law and Jewish Order. The Old Testament God is to be feared. But he was the promise of survival for his wandering people if they obeyed

His commandments. The Old Testament God was the right God for the right people at the right time. However, with the appearance of Jesus Christ, the Good News was made known for the benefit of all humanity and His Gospel of Truth is pointing the way to a new reality. He is giving humanity a new understanding of God. Gone is the Mosaic God of retribution and *his* replacement is a Christian God of never-ending love. Jesus Christ is all about the reality of unconditional love (agape). By virtue of His sacrifice, the Christ Spirit has permeated our souls with His love. Just as the Living Christ is within us, we are also within Him. And His Gospel is written upon our hearts. We need only to urgently seek this love as some of the Gnostics did so long ago.

The message of Christ *is* the Gospel of Truth, and it is important to remember that Jesus Christ was the greatest heretic of them all. In the Gospels of the New Testament, we are told of the many times that Jesus Christ confronted the powerful religious leaders of His day. Jesus Christ was in possession of the truth, as revealed to Him by God. In contrast to the wisdom of Christ, many of the worldly religious leaders and scribes were—much like many of the religious leaders today—in possession of empty pretensions. During the life of Jesus Christ, the men who sought to control the keys to heaven were actually blocking the path to the kingdom of heaven. And Jesus Christ was not timid in telling them so: "But woe to you, scribes and Pharisees, hypocrites! For you shut up the kingdom of heaven against men; for you neither go in yourselves, nor do you allow those who are entering to go in." (Matthew 23:13) Has this condition significantly changed in our world today? As an advanced spirit from the highest order, Jesus Christ was sent forth to liberate us from our ignorance. He was keenly aware that His message represented a major change from the old ways to a new way of living, and this understanding is expressed in the Gospels: "For I say to you, that unless your righteousness exceeds the righteousness of the scribes and Pharisees, you will by no means enter the kingdom of heaven." (Matthew 5:20) Since the days when Jesus Christ walked the earth, organized religion has changed very little. With their need to acquire power and authority, many of the religious leaders today possess the same old desires for material acquisition, and they display the same intolerance and hypocrisy.

Throughout the ages, the Great Church has employed extreme measures to hide the rebellious nature of Jesus Christ from us, and for reasons they know best. The Church has a vested interest in minimizing the rebellious aspects of Jesus Christ because this information threatens their authority. I find it strange and ironic that the very institution, which claims Jesus Christ as their God and founder, would be the same institution that has acted in a manner identical to the religious and political institutions that condemned their founder, i.e. the Sanhedrin and the Roman government. If any organization on earth should have known the dangers of arbitrary persecution, it should have been the Roman Church. But institutional self-preservation and the acquisition of power (power equals authority) has been the driving force behind the development of our Christian institutions. They believe it is not possible to maintain their authority if they provide a religious platform that allows reasonable people to debate their agenda. By resorting to absolute authority, the Church has effectively prevented any discussion of dissent about their accepted creeds and doctrines. It is not in the Church's vested interest to reveal the rebellious aspect of Jesus Christ.

With savage brutality, the Church has sent many pious men and women of Christian faith to the fires of vengeance for nothing more than being devout Christians. The slaughter of the Cathars during the thirteenth century by the Roman Church is certainly an example of this kind of violent repression. The untold misery caused by the Inquisition rivals any of the horror stories of the twentieth century. And we are still living with the hatred and violence caused by Pope Urban's call for a "holy war" against the Muslims in the Middle East during the eleventh century. The pope's call for this "holy war" resulted in decades of massacres that historians have named the Crusades. By brutally crushing all dissent, the Roman Church could not, at the same time, extol this same dissentious behavior in their founder.

During the sixteenth century, after the Reformation, the Protestants would get busy with developing their techniques of persecution too. Although there has been a litany of moral crimes committed against humanity by the Protestants, these nefarious acts have often escaped our moral outrage due to their shorter period of duration. The Roman Catholics had more time to perfect their techniques of torture. It does appear that every time men have approached the words of love spoken by the man from Galilee, they have ignored or distorted His message. Consequently, most of the truth about Jesus Christ has been buried under meaningless words and obscure doctrines. While traveling on our spiritual journey, we shall move beyond the diluted and distorted representation of Jesus Christ. If we earnestly seek the truth, we will find the true Christ.

Fortunately, the true Christ is alive and in our hearts. His words are alive in the Gospels, including the Gospels that were excluded from the New Testament Bible Canon. His message is within reach for all who earnestly seek it. We have no need to depend on any institution for our understanding of the message of Christ, and we certainly do not need clerical middle-men telling us what we should or should not believe. Our Christian institutions are not the source of our salvation. When we gather in fellowship or congregate to share the love and faith of Jesus Christ with each other, it is, indeed, a very glorious occasion. But we shall always remember that the authority we seek is found in the spirit of Christ. His love is the source of our salvation. The Christ Spirit can be found in our prayers, meditations, and intuitions. But this spirit can also be found in our art, music and literature. The exalted spirit of Christ, like the spirit of God, can be found everywhere if our hearts honestly seek Him. We may fervently strive to find satisfaction in our physical world by trying to possess more material things or by having a greater accumulation of wealth and power. But it will *all* come to naught if we deny the true nature of who we are. Our true being is our human spirit, and this is the force that animates our physical body. And God has created Christ to be the Savior for our human spirit. Until we realize that we reside in Christ and He resides within us, we will be consigned to the darkness of the physical world.

By His appearance on earth, the Christ Spirit has entered into humanity. This means that He is personally within each one of us. The Christ within us provides us with the unique opportunity to develop a personal relationship with Christ. God the Father is the first cause of all that we see and know. At this time in our spiritual evolution, God is unknowable to us. Fortunately, the Christ Spirit is an entity that we can know and relate to. We know that He understands our human condition because He lived here amongst us. Through the experience of living in the corporeal body of Jesus of Nazareth, the Christ Spirit gave us a very special gift. He has provided us with the unique ability to have our own personal relationship with Him. We can identify with the humanity of Jesus of Nazareth. We can also find our way into the kingdom of heaven by crossing the spiritual bridge that has been given to us by the Christ Spirit. And this bridge is constructed from our thoughts of love. Again, I must add that the man Jesus of Nazareth, in whom the divine spirit of Christ did dwell, was a very special human being. As we learned earlier in our journey, his spiritual evolution as a human being has far exceeded the level of spiritual growth achieved by all of humanity. And it was this spiritual achievement that allowed Jesus to be the vehicle for the Christ Spirit. As such, Jesus is a unique man who is certainly worthy of our most sincere love, devotion and adulation.

In working together, the man Jesus and the divine spirit of Christ gave us the greatest gift of love humanity has ever known. This gift enables us to go within ourselves to find the spirit of Christ. We will find salvation from within ourselves. The search for Christ is an inward search, not an outward search. Christ will only be found within the human heart. By finding the love of Christ within our hearts, we can surmount all obstacles in our path. Jesus Christ made His love available to us through His sacrifice for humanity, and we will discover that His love is intrinsic to our heart. He is knocking on our door—and we all have the choice to open it. In the Gospels, Jesus Christ instructs us to have our heart in the "right place" and, then, the "details will take care of themselves." The right place for our hearts is in His love. Love is the answer to all questions about living together with all of God's creation.

On a practical level, this means we are to develop our love and compassion—as we apprehend the love and compassion evinced by Jesus Christ. With such love in our minds and hearts, we will, consequently, begin to express this love in *every* situation. All of humanity's great problems—such as the issue of abortion; the plague of racism; the greed that depredates our earth and converts our corporations into self-serving entities; the lack of food in various indigent regions of the world; the violence and hatred that engenders war; the seemingly insoluble conflict between people of different nations—will *all* be solved, if we are able to manifest the unconditional love Christ has for each one of us. If we believe this to be a naïve assessment, then we do not *really* understand the power of His love. It is completely essential to our spiritual journey to understand the power of love, as expressed by Christ, and to embody our thoughts with this powerful love. It is to be duly noted again; the concept of Christian love is not for the frivolous minded. It is the power of God Almighty. And, like the philosopher's stone, this powerful love will transform us into heavenly beings. Our only limitation will be our inability to discover and develop the type of love that characterizes God the Father. This is the type of love shown to us by Jesus Christ.

Certainly, one of the more misleading doctrines created by the Great Church is the deification of Jesus Christ into God. By mandating that Jesus Christ *is* God, the humanity of Jesus Christ was lost. I believe it was this loss of humanity that the pious priest Arius was hoping to avoid so many years ago by his understanding that the "Son" was created by the "Father." By converting the Son *into* the Father, the Church has done itself a great disservice. It should be noted that Saint Paul, as the first Christian theologian and reputed founder of Christianity, did not believe that Jesus Christ was God incarnate, and he never avowed such a belief. It seems the early Church leaders were intent upon ignoring the very words of their true Founder. In the Gospel of John we will find the statement: "For God so loved the world that he gave his one and only Son, that whoever believes in him shall not perish but have eternal life." (John 3:16) As we saw earlier, the phrase "Son of God" is a spiritual metaphor, and it is understandable to our human minds. In this Gospel passage, John is not saying Christ is the Father, rather he is saying that Christ is the Son. And, as we have seen in our other gospel examples, the phrase "Son of God" was used by Jesus Christ Himself. Because the Church has insisted that we believe in the doctrine of "Jesus Christ *is* God," we may begin to understand why millions of people are turning away from the Church's door. With our rational minds, we suspect that we are being misled by this doctrine, and our suspicions are preventing us from discovering and understanding the true nature of Jesus Christ.

As human beings we need a theology that includes human factors that we can relate to and understand. God is beyond the understanding of men and women and, as such, is a remote and unknowable reality to us. But we can relate to Jesus Christ because there is a human element in His story. The Christ Spirit was aware of our human needs, and this is why He came to live amongst us in the body of a man. As an advanced divine spirit, the Christ Spirit could have chosen any form of expression. For example, He could have manifested Himself as an angel, but He chose to come as a man. We will not find any examples of Jesus Christ openly declaring doctrines about His divinity in the New Testament. The "Jesus Christ is God" doctrine was created by *men* for the reasons we encountered earlier in our journey. Jesus Christ was both human and divine—and we should be content to leave it at this description. As stated earlier in our journey, the real nature of Jesus Christ is difficult for most human minds to ponder due to our current stage of spiritual development. With our new understanding of Jesus Christ, our spiritual awareness will begin to elevate and more shall be revealed.

Our homecoming is, as Homer allegorically illustrated in his *Odyssey*, fraught with many dangers. We begin our journey with an exploration into our deep unconscious where the arcane storms of Poseidon rage and other chimerical monsters threaten us with our fear. As we have seen, our fears are within our mind, and many of them remain hidden from our awareness. Like brave Odysseus, we must be willing to navigate the treacherous waters of our unconscious to confront our fears where they live. Our spiritual journey will take us through the world of desire where the power of Calypso calls us into indulgent sensuality. If we are unwilling to confront our hidden fears and selfish desires, we will be unable to refine our behavior, and we shall become shipwrecked souls on the shores of perdition.

In our journey home, we seek the knowledge (Gnosis) of Hermes so that we can free ourselves from the shackles that are binding us to the material world. We will be ever vigilant to prevent behavior that will convert us into "swine" and we must avoid the "lotus" of forgetfulness, which conceals the vision of our true home with illusions of self-satisfaction. To be worthy of our homecoming, we will also need to navigate through the temptations of Hades. And, if we are to find our way home, we will need to steer clear of the Sirens with their deceptive songs, providing us with the false reality of death. Oh! Sweet and loyal Penelope, where art thee? Indeed, we will face many dangers in our journey back home but with the "Holy Moly" from heaven, we shall arrive at our destination.

In *The Odyssey*, Homer reveals a fundamental principle that is essential to our spiritual homecoming. While attempting to return home to his beloved wife Penelope and to his mythical Isle of Ithaca, Odysseus lost all his men to death, and he found himself alone on his journey to return home. As we seek the spiritual knowledge (Gnosis) in the message of Christ, we must, on our own accord, direct our hearts to Jesus Christ. Our search for truth is a personal search, and it will be the *individual* who owns the responsibility for the work that needs to be done. It is not possible for another person or institution to do this work for us. Certainly, we shall meet special individuals who can offer us directions for our journey home. These spiritual guides may assist us in finding the correct path, but, ultimately, it is entirely up to us as individuals to find the love of Christ in our hearts and to practice this love in our life.

In realizing the love of Jesus Christ in our daily awareness, we are experiencing the spirit of Christ. I think of this revelation as a second resurrection of Christ. This is our personal resurrection of Christ, and He is manifesting within our own consciousness. This is similar to Paul's mystical experience of Christ. When we become Christ-oriented, we will undergo a profound transformation, and our world will be changed forever. The love that is in Christ will fill our hearts, minds, and souls. This is the true meaning of being re-born. And this spiritual transformation cannot be faked, nor can it be purchased with our money. We will know the re-born individual by the love and compassion that he or she has for everyone—without exception. What we seek is nothing less than the immediacy of the Christ within us. As the fourteenth-century mystic Meister Eckhart reminded us, we must be reborn in the spirit of Christ throughout our day—each and every day. It is not a one time commitment. The love of Christ is the love of God. This is our promise of a world where our actions will be based upon empathy, understanding and love.

No experience more profoundly touches the human heart than the intensely burning flame of the religious experience. This visceral encounter with God is our "burning bush." Humanity's numinous experiences of God have been the source for much of our most exquisite expressions of mysticism, art, literature, music and architecture. And these religious experiences have also created the most sublime, beautiful and admirable expressions of love, as manifested by such individuals as Mother Teresa of Calcutta and Dr Martin Luther King, Jr. While our world is in urgent need of greater love, we may still find many splendid examples of individuals who are practicing the self-sacrificing love of Jesus Christ. In their efforts to improve the lives of a few, these individuals are actually helping to improve the whole of humanity. If any of our brothers and sisters is in pain, how can we *afford* to ignore their plight? And it is not necessary for compassionate people to call themselves Christians. They may not even know Jesus Christ. It does not matter what we call ourselves. Our goal is to extend self-sacrificing and unconditional love to humanity because this love *is* the spirit of Christ.

Unfortunately, this same type of religious experience has also brought many men and women to their moral and spiritual destruction. How we react to our religious epiphanies will depend upon how we construct our thoughts about God in our mind. Any architect will tell us that even the most sublime drawing of a building will come to naught if only the cheapest materials are used in the construction of the building. Likewise, if we experience the sublime idea of God in our mind and we, then, build this idea into thought patterns using only the base material of our lowest desires, our thoughts about God will *not* lead us in a Godly direction. As we learned earlier in our journey, our mind resides in The World of Thought and—remembering the Hermetic axiom "as above, so below"—this world functions in a similar fashion to our physical world. If we are to effectively build loving thoughts about God in our mind, we are to utilize only the thought material of the highest quality when constructing our thoughts about God. In the physical world, we can choose to build an object from lead or we can choose to build it from gold. In the World of Thought, we can similarly choose to build our thoughts with ignoble materials such as the desires of greed and selfishness or we can choose to build our thoughts with the spiritual material of divine love. This *is* the wisdom Jesus Christ is referring to when He instructs us to love God and to love our neighbors. If we utilize our love for God in our thinking, all things are possible. Human beings will become Christ-like when they are constructing their thought forms by building these thoughts with only the finest material available in the World of Thought. And the finest material available is the love expressed by Jesus Christ. Thoughts of love, empathy and compassion are composed of Christ-Love, and they reflect our most beautiful and most harmonious spiritual thoughts. These are the thoughts that manifest the love Christ has for all of us. This love is God.

Our ego is often our biggest impediment to understanding the message of Christ. It will be our own selves that obstruct our path to spiritual growth and, consequently, we will be preventing our own homecoming. This is why Jesus Christ is instructing us to be childlike when seeking the truth in His message. The spiritual mind is a mind that is unencumbered by the need or desire to prove that its truth is the *only* truth required by all people. We all walk our own existential path—and we alone are responsible for making sense of our world. We are seekers, like the Gnostics of old, and we are looking to discover our path to the truth. While I sincerely hope that others have found some edification and enlightenment on our spiritual journey, I am aware that my truth has been derived from my own personal experiences in life. Hopefully, I do pray the information collected on our journey was of some assistance to all of those who made this journey with me. We can take what seemed to fit, and leave the rest for another day. The important thing is to keep an open mind. Finding the spiritual treasure of truth is an ongoing process and our continuing journey will certainly take us along many different pathways. However, if we are able to get out of our own way, we will understand that Christ purveys the truth for *all seekers*. If we manifest the love expressed by Jesus Christ, we will experience amazing spiritual development and *all* of our problems will soon disappear. With our humble attempts, we seek to understand His truth, knowing that, as humans, our understanding will be imperfect. But by having the Christ Spirit at the center of our being, we will begin to effectively remove our ego from its excessive interference in our thinking. I think Saint Francis of Assisi said it best; "Above all the grace and the gifts that Christ gives to his beloved is that of overcoming self."

May we all overcome the self by living in the rays of truth that emanate from our Savior, Jesus Christ! Surely, we will discover that, as we continue our journey, we are truly one in God and we will come to know that God is within *all* of us. We can and will look ahead to the year 2012 and beyond with great anticipation for the arrival of a new beginning. As children of God, our blessing from our Father is for us to know peace, love, and harmony. This is the gift that Jesus Christ speaks about in *all* the Gospels. As this phase of our journey comes to an end, I find it fitting to close with the words of the beloved Meister Eckhart: "All God wants of man is a peaceful heart." This is what we desire too.

Thank you for traveling on this journey with me and we will meet again in the universal kinship. With a new understanding of love, our eyes will open and we shall all know true Christianity. Peace and goodwill shall prevail upon the earth. Let us all remember that God is blessing us, and do keep the faith.

Appendix:
The Allegory of the Cave

The following allegory can be found in Plato's dialogue, *The Republic*. This translation is by Benjamin Jowett (Anchor Books, 1960) from his book entitled *The Republic and Other Works*. The format included here is a reproduction from the website:

http://www.historyguide.org/intellect/allegory.html

A gracious "thank you" is extended to Dr. Steven Kreis for granting his permission to reproduce his website in this current work. His web portal has other attractions too.

This allegory is in the form of a dialogue between Socrates and Glaucon. This was the preferred form of literary expression used by Plato. As you read the description of the cave, it may be useful to sketch a diagram of what the cave looks like on a piece of paper to conceptualize how the prisoners and the background light are arranged in the cave.

[**Socrates**] And now, I said, let me show in a figure how far our nature is enlightened or unenlightened: Behold! Human beings living in an underground cave, which has a mouth open towards the light and reaching all along the cave; here they have been from their childhood, and have their legs and necks chained so that they cannot move, and can only see before them, being prevented by the chains from turning round their heads.

Above and behind them a fire is blazing at a distance, and between the fire and the prisoners there is a raised way; and you will see, if you look, a low wall built along the way, like the screen which marionette players have in front of them, over which they show the puppets.

[**Glaucon**] I see.

[**Socrates**] And do you see, I said, men passing along the wall carrying all sorts of vessels, and statues and figures of animals made of wood and stone and various materials, which appear over the wall? Some of them are talking, others silent.

[**Glaucon**] You have shown me a strange image, and they are strange prisoners.

[**Socrates**] Like ourselves, I replied; and they see only their own shadows, or the shadows of one another, which the fire throws on the opposite wall of the cave?

[**Glaucon**] True, he said; how could they see anything but the shadows if they were never allowed to move their heads?

[**Socrates**] And of the objects which are being carried in like manner they would only see the shadows?

[**Glaucon**] Yes, he said.

[**Socrates**] And if they were able to converse with one another, would they not suppose that they were naming what was actually before them?

[**Glaucon**] Very true.

[**Socrates**] And suppose further that the prison had an echo which came from the other side, would they not be sure to fancy when one of the passers-by spoke that the voice which they heard came from the passing shadow?

[**Glaucon**] No question, he replied.

[**Socrates**] To them, I said, the truth would be literally nothing but the shadows of the images.

[**Glaucon**] That is certain.

[**Socrates**] And now look again, and see what will naturally follow if the prisoners are released and disabused of their error. At first, when any of them is liberated and compelled suddenly to stand up and turn his neck round and walk and look towards the light, he will suffer sharp pains; the glare will distress him, and he will be unable to see the realities of which in his former state he had seen the shadows; and then conceive someone saying to him, that what he saw before was an illusion, but that now, when he is approaching nearer to being and his eye is turned towards more real existence, he has a clearer vision, what will be his reply? And you may further imagine that his instructor is pointing to the objects as they pass and requiring him to name them, will he not be perplexed? Will he not fancy that the shadows which he formerly saw are truer than the objects which are now shown to him?

[**Glaucon**] Far truer.

[**Socrates**] And if he is compelled to look straight at the light, will he not have a pain in his eyes which will make him turn away to take and take in the objects of vision which he can see, and which he will conceive to be in reality clearer than the things which are now being shown to him?

[**Glaucon**] True, he now.

[**Socrates**] And suppose once more, that he is reluctantly dragged up a steep and rugged ascent, and held fast until he's forced into the presence of the sun himself, is he not likely to be pained and irritated? When he approaches the light his eyes will be dazzled, and he will not be able to see anything at all of what are now called realities.

[**Glaucon**] Not all in a moment, he said.

[**Socrates**] He will require to grow accustomed to the sight of the upper world. And first he will see the shadows best, next the reflections of men and other objects in the water, and then the objects themselves; then he will gaze upon the light of the moon and the stars and the spangled heaven; and he will see the sky and the stars by night better than the sun or the light of the sun by day?

[**Glaucon**] Certainly.

[**Socrates**] Last of he will be able to see the sun, and not mere reflections of him in the water, but he will see him in his own proper place, and not in another; and he will contemplate him as he is.

[**Glaucon**] Certainly.

[**Socrates**] He will then proceed to argue that this is he who gives the season and the years, and is the guardian of all that is in the visible world, and in a certain way the cause of all things which he and his fellows have been accustomed to behold?

[**Glaucon**] Clearly, he said, he would first see the sun and then reason about him.

[**Socrates**] And when he remembered his old habitation, and the wisdom of the cave and his fellow prisoners, do you not suppose that he would felicitate himself on the change, and pity them?

[**Glaucon**] Certainly, he would.

[**Socrates**] And if they were in the habit of conferring honors among themselves on those who were quickest to observe the passing shadows and to remark which of them went before, and which followed after, and which were together; and who were therefore best able to draw conclusions as to the future, do you think that he would care for such honors and glories, or envy the possessors of them? Would he not say with Homer,

Better to be the poor servant of a poor master, and to endure anything, rather than think as they do and live after their manner?

[**Glaucon**] Yes, he said, I think that he would rather suffer anything than entertain these false notions and live in this miserable manner.

[**Socrates**] Imagine once more, I said, such an one coming suddenly out of the sun to be replaced in his old situation; would he not be certain to have his eyes full of darkness?

[**Glaucon**] To be sure, he said.

[**Socrates**] And if there were a contest, and he had to compete in measuring the shadows with the prisoners who had never moved out of the cave, while his sight was still weak, and before his eyes had become steady (and the time which would be needed to acquire this new habit of sight might be very considerable) would he not be ridiculous? Men would say of him that up he went and down he came without his eyes; and that it was better not even to think of ascending; and if any one tried to loose another and lead him up to the light, let them only catch the offender, and they would put him to death.

[**Glaucon**] No question, he said.

[**Socrates**] This entire allegory, I said, you may now append, dear Glaucon, to the previous argument; the prison-house is the world of sight, the light of the fire is the sun, and you will not misapprehend me if you interpret the journey upwards to be the ascent of the soul into the intellectual world according to my poor belief, which, at your desire, I have expressed whether rightly or wrongly God knows. But, whether true or false, my opinion is that in the world of knowledge the idea of good appears last of all, and is seen only with an effort; and, when seen, is also inferred to be the universal author of all things beautiful and right, parent of light and of the lord of light in this visible world, and the immediate source of reason and truth in the intellectual; and that this is the power upon which he who would act rationally, either in public or private life must have his eye fixed.

[**Glaucon**] I agree, he said, as far as I am able to understand you.

[**Socrates**] Moreover, I said, you must not wonder that those who attain to this beatific vision are unwilling to descend to human affairs; for their souls are ever hastening into the upper world where they desire to dwell; which desire of theirs is very natural, if our allegory may be trusted.

[**Glaucon**] Yes, very natural.

[**Socrates**] And is there anything surprising in one who passes from divine contemplations to the evil state of man, misbehaving himself in a ridiculous manner; if, while his eyes are blinking and before he has become accustomed to the surrounding darkness, he is compelled to fight in courts of law, or in other places, about the images or the shadows of images of justice, and is endeavoring to meet the conceptions of those who have never yet seen absolute justice?

[**Glaucon**] Anything but surprising, he replied.

[**Socrates**] Any one who has common sense will remember that the bewilderments of the eyes are of two kinds, and arise from two causes, either from coming out of the light or from going into the light, which is true of the mind's eye, quite as much as of the bodily eye; and he who remembers this when he sees any one whose vision is perplexed and weak, will not be too ready to laugh; he will first ask whether that soul of man has come out of the brighter light, and is unable to see because unaccustomed to the dark, or having turned from darkness to the day is dazzled by excess of light. And he will count the one happy in his condition and state of being, and he will pity the other; or, if he have a mind to laugh at the soul which comes from below into the light, there will be more reason in this than in the laugh which greets him who returns from above out of the light into the cave.

[**Glaucon**] That, he said, is a very just distinction.

[**Socrates**] But then, if I am right, certain professors of education must be wrong when they say that they can put a knowledge into the soul which was not there before, like sight into blind eyes.

[**Glaucon**] They undoubtedly say this, he replied.

[**Socrates**] Whereas, our argument shows that the power and capacity of learning exists in the soul already; and that just as the eye was unable to turn from darkness to light without the whole body, so too the instrument of knowledge can only by the movement of the whole soul be turned from the world of becoming into that of being, and learn by degrees to endure the sight of being, and of the brightest and best of being, or in other words, of the good.

[**Glaucon**] Very true.

[**Socrates**] And must there not be some art which will effect conversion in the easiest and quickest manner; not implanting the faculty of sight, for that exists already, but has been turned in the wrong direction, and is looking away from the truth?

[**Glaucon**] Yes, he said, such an art may be presumed.

[**Socrates**] And whereas the other so-called virtues of the soul seem to be akin to bodily qualities, for even when they are not originally innate they can be implanted later by habit and exercise, the of wisdom more than anything else contains a divine element which always remains, and by this conversion is rendered useful and profitable; or, on the other hand, hurtful and useless. Did you never observe the narrow intelligence flashing from the keen eye of a clever rogue—how eager he is, how clearly his paltry soul sees the way to his end; he is the reverse of blind, but his keen eyesight is forced into the service of evil, and he is mischievous in proportion to his cleverness.

[**Glaucon**] Very true, he said.

[**Socrates**] But what if there had been a circumcision of such natures in the days of their youth; and they had been severed from those sensual pleasures, such as eating and drinking, which, like leaden weights, were attached to them at their birth, and which drag them down and turn the vision of their souls upon the things that are below—if, I say, they had been released from these impediments and turned in the opposite direction, the very same faculty in them would have seen the truth as keenly as they see what their eyes are turned to now.

[**Glaucon**] Very likely.

[**Socrates**] Yes, I said; and there is another thing which is likely. or rather a necessary inference from what has preceded, that neither the uneducated and uninformed of the truth, nor yet those who never make an end of their education, will be able ministers of State; not the former, because they have no single aim of duty which is the rule of all their actions, private as well as public; nor the latter, because they will not act at all except upon compulsion, fancying that they are already dwelling apart in the islands of the blest.

[**Glaucon**] Very true, he replied.

[**Socrates**] Then, I said, the business of us who are the founders of the State will be to compel the best minds to attain that knowledge which we have already shown to be the greatest of all—they must continue to ascend until they arrive at the good; but when they have ascended and seen enough we must not allow them to do as they do now.

[**Glaucon**] What do you mean?

[**Socrates**] I mean that they remain in the upper world: but this must not be allowed; they must be made to descend again among the prisoners in the cave, and partake of their labors and honors, whether they are worth having or not.

[**Glaucon**] But is not this unjust? he said; ought we to give them a worse life, when they might have a better?

[**Socrates**] You have again forgotten, my friend, I said, the intention of the legislator, who did not aim at making any one class in the State happy above the rest; the happiness was to be in the whole State, and he held the citizens together by persuasion and necessity, making them benefactors of the State, and therefore benefactors of one another; to this end he created them, not to please themselves, but to be his instruments in binding up the State.

[**Glaucon**] True, he said, I had forgotten.

[**Socrates**] Observe, Glaucon, that there will be no injustice in compelling our philosophers to have a care and providence of others; we shall explain to them that in other States, men of their class are not obliged to share in the toils of politics: and this is reasonable, for they grow up at their own sweet will, and the government would rather not have them. Being self-taught, they cannot be expected to show any gratitude for a culture which they have never received. But we have brought you into the world to be rulers of the hive, kings of yourselves and of the other citizens, and have educated you far better and more perfectly than they have been educated, and you are better able to share in the double duty. Wherefore each of you, when his turn comes, must go down to the general underground abode, and get the habit of seeing in the dark. When you have acquired the habit, you will see ten thousand times better than the inhabitants of the cave, and you will know what the several images are, and what they represent, because you have seen the beautiful and just and good in their truth. And thus our State which is also yours will be a reality, and not a dream only, and will be administered in a spirit unlike that of other States, in which men fight with one another about shadows only and are distracted in the struggle for power, which in their eyes is a great good. Whereas the truth is that the State in which the rulers are most reluctant to govern is always the best and most quietly governed, and the State in which they are most eager, the worst.

[**Glaucon**] Quite true, he replied.

[**Socrates**] And will our pupils, when they hear this, refuse to take their turn at the toils of State, when they are allowed to spend the greater part of their time with one another in the heavenly light?

[**Glaucon**] Impossible, he answered; for they are just men, and the commands which we impose upon them are just; there can be no doubt that every one of them will take office as a stern necessity, and not after the fashion of our present rulers of State.

[**Socrates**] Yes, my friend, I said; and there lies the point. You must contrive for your future rulers another and a better life than that of a ruler, and then you may have a well-ordered State; for only in the State which offers this, will they rule who are truly rich, not in silver and gold, but in virtue and wisdom, which are the true blessings of life. Whereas if they go to the administration of public affairs, poor and hungering after the' own private advantage, thinking that hence they are to snatch the chief good, order there can never be; for they will be fighting about office, and the civil and domestic broils which thus arise will be the ruin of the rulers themselves and of the whole State.

[**Glaucon**] Most true, he replied.

[**Socrates**] And the only life which looks down upon the life of political ambition is that of true philosophy. Do you know of any other?

[**Glaucon**] Indeed, I do not, he said.

[**Socrates**] And those who govern ought not to be lovers of the task? For, if they are, there will be rival lovers, and they will fight.

[**Glaucon**] No question.

[**Socrates**] Who then are those whom we shall compel to be guardians? Surely they will be the men who are wisest about affairs of State, and by whom the State is best administered, and who at the same time have other honors and another and a better life than that of politics?

[**Glaucon**] They are the men, and I will choose them, he replied.

[**Socrates**] And now shall we consider in what way such guardians will be produced, and how they are to be brought from darkness to light—as some are said to have ascended from the world below to the gods?

[**Glaucon**] By all means, he replied.

[**Socrates**] The process, I said, is not the turning over of an oyster shell, but the turning round of a soul passing from a day which is little better than night to the true day of being, that is, the ascent from below, which we affirm to be true philosophy?

[**Glaucon**] Quite so.

Bibliography

Armstrong, Karen, *A History of God* (Ballantine Books, 1993)

Brakke, David, *The Gnostics: Myth, Ritual, and Diversity* (Harvard University Press, 2010)

Capra, Fritjof, *The Tao of Physics* (Bantam Books, 1984)

Churton, Tobias, *The Gnostics* (Barns & Noble Books, 1987)

Frankl, Viktor E., *Man's Search for Meaning* (Beacon Press, 2006)

Hall, Calvin S. & Norby, Vernon J., *A Primer of Jungian Psychology* (A Mentor Book, 1973)

Hall, Manly P., *Twelve World Teachers* (Philosophical Research Society, 1965)

Jung, C.G., *Memories, Dreams, Reflections*, Edited by Aniela Jaffe, Translation by Richard and Clara Winston (Vintage Books, 1963)

King, Karen L., *What is Gnosticism* (Belknap Press of Harvard University Press, 2005)

Lederman, Leon & Teresi, Dick, *The God Particle: If the Universe is the Answer, What is the Question* (Mariner Books, 2006)

Meyer, Marvin, *The Gnostic Discoveries* (Harper San Francisco, 2005)

Nigg, Walter, *The Heretics*, Translation by Richard and Clara Winston (Alfred A. Knopf, Inc., 1962)

O'Grady, Joan, *Early Christian Heresies* (Barns & Noble Books, 1985)

Pagels, Elaine, *Beyond Belief: The Secret Gospel of Thomas* (Vintage Books, 2004)

Plato, *The Republic and Other Works*, Translation by Benjamin Jowett (Anchor Books, 1960)

Sahakian, William S., *History of Philosophy* (Barns & Noble Books, 1968).

Singh, Simon, *Big Bang: The Origin of the Universe* (Harper Perennial Books, 2005)

Szaaz, Thomas S., *The Myth of Mental Illness: Foundations of a Theory of Personal Conduct* (Harper Perennial; Anv edition 2010)

The Nag Hammadi Scriptures, The Revised and Updated Translation of Sacred Gnostic Texts, Edited by Marvin Meyer (HarperOne, 2007)

The Oxford Illustrated History of Christianity, Edited by John McManners (Oxford University Press, 1992)

Walker, Ethan, *The Mystic Christ* (Devi Press 2003)

About the Author

J. Craig Woods served in the US Navy and attended the University of California, majoring in psychology and philosophy. He is an ordained minister and the author of "A New Age of Vision." He has worked as a Unix System Engineer for the last twenty years. Throughout his entire life, he has had an abiding interest in the spiritual development of humanity.